# BASIC BUDGETING WORKBOOK

*Apostle Elishaphat*

iUniverse, Inc.
New York   Bloomington

**Basic Budgeting Workbook**

iUniverse books may be ordered through booksellers or by contacting:

iUniverse
1663 Liberty Drive
Bloomington, IN 47403
www.iuniverse.com
1-800-Authors (1-800-288-4677)

Because of the dynamic nature of the Internet, any Web addresses or links contained in this book may have changed since publication and may no longer be valid. The views expressed in this work are solely those of the author and do not necessarily reflect the views of the publisher, and the publisher hereby disclaims any responsibility for them.

ISBN: 978-1-4502-4951-5 (sc)
ISBN: 978-1-4502-4953-9 (ebook)
ISBN: 978-1-4502-4952-2 (hc)

Printed in the United States of America

iUniverse rev. date: 10/26/2010

# BASIC BUDGETING WORKBOOK

## DEDICATION

This book is dedicated to all those who are faced with everyday expenses that, if not controlled, will hinder their desire to stay out of debt.

# Contents

# FOREWORD

This book is designed to be brief, *easy to use* and the result is guaranteed to be accurate and satisfactory once followed as instructed.

You may have goals and dreams, but if you don't set up a financial guideline, you may not reach them. That is why I am suggesting this "budgeting plan" as a financial guide to help its user attain his or her goals.

In order to expedite your budgeting journey to a better financial life, it is recommended that you carefully read and follow *all* the instructions provided herein.

# ABOUT THE AUTHOR

The author of this budgeting book is Apostle Elishaphat, who specializes in the field of financial counseling and budgeting. He has traveled extensively throughout many countries and spoke in many seminars and organizations on the subject. The Apostle has worked closely with numerous accountants to improve the financial lives of many (both Christian and non-Christian), some of whom were faced with serious credit delinquency and outstanding financial debt. He has also helped numerous families across the United States and Canada to structure wise spending habits toward a better financial future. Other than reaching out to help someone in need, counseling has been one of the Apostle's strongest attributes, and the ability to find solutions for difficult situations and organizing are some key virtues he has portrayed. The Apostle's utmost passion is to travel throughout the world to help as many poor, sick, hungry, and homeless people as possible, and he believes he will continue to do so, until he goes the way of all flesh. Some family members and close friends have criticized him for reaching out to help others in need, but those criticisms were powerless to stop him. What is in his heart is from God, and cannot be removed by mankind.

# Endorsement

Congratulations! Your decision to purchase this book is one of the wisest decisions you have made. The knowledge you will gain from reading this book will increase your wisdom. The application of this book will increase your power—power to win financially.

Do you know how to use your paycheck wisely for today and for your future? Where do you stand financially? Are you living in debt? Are you aware of how much interest, fees, and charges you are paying monthly in keeping your debt? Are you in an endless cycle of finance and refinance? Are you building assets or liabilities? Do the answers to these questions make you feel stressed out and worried about your future?

Times have been uncertain. The more you consume, the more you are hurting and the more you are confused. Debts, bankruptcy, poor savings habits, and job insecurity can create situations of stress in your home. However, you can change this situation around if you learn and apply the principles and use this workbook as designed. Then, your next step would be to learn *the principles of tax saving strategies*, obtain and apply knowledge of how to make your money work harder for you, and apply strategies now to become financially independent. Don't gamble with your future! Which situation would you rather be in at age sixty-five—dead, dead broke, still working, or financially independent? You can choose to shape your future. The time to start is now! To begin, read this book, apply the principles, and use the pages in the workbook provided.

I once heard someone say: "Excuses are tools for the incompetent building bridges that go nowhere that result in monuments of nothingness". Don't reach age sixty-five and be dead broke or still working. At every age in life, some people always find excuses as to why they cannot start saving. Do you find yourself using any of these excuses?

**Age 18 to 25**: "Me, save and invest? Are you kidding? I'm just getting my education. You can't expect me to be able to invest now. I'm young, and I want to have a good time. After all, I'll be in college for a year or so. If and when I get out of college, I'll start investing."

**Age 25 to 35**: "You don't expect me to save and invest now, do you? Remember, I've only been working a few years. Things will be looking up soon, and then I'll be able to invest. Right now, I have to dress well in order to make a good impression. Wait till I'm a little older. There's plenty of time."

**Age 35 to 45**: "How can I save and invest now? Married with children to care for, I never had so many expenses in my life. When the children are a little older, I can start thinking about investing."

**Age 45 to 55**: "I wish I could save and invest now, but I just can't do it. I have two children in college, and it's taking every cent and then some to keep them there. I've had to go into debt the last few years to meet the college bills. But that won't last forever, and then I can start investing."

**Age 55 to 65**: "I know I should be saving and investing now, but money is tight. It's not so easy for a person my age to better him or herself. All I can do is hang on. Why didn't I start to save and invest twenty years ago? Well, maybe something will turn up."

**Age Over 65**: "Yes, it's too late now. We are living with our eldest son. It isn't so nice, but what else can we do? We have social security, but who can live on that? If only I had saved a little and invested when I had the money. You can't invest after there is no income."

So how do you get to financial independence? Here is what I believe will get you there:

1. **Start budgeting**: If you hate the word *budget*, then change it to *spending plan*. Use this workbook!

2. **Start saving at least 10 percent of your income for retirement**: Give some, save some, and spend some. You keep working and paying everyone else. What about you? Everyone else is making their financial goals off of your money. Shouldn't you get paid too?

3. **Save in a smart place**: It is important to know where to put your money so that you have the greatest tax reduction benefits, you outpace inflation, and your principle can be secured. Can you get all three benefits in one place? It is very possible.

4. **Don't cash out retirement plans:** Once you start saving, don't touch your savings funds. Treat that money like a bill you just paid. The name on the bill is *my future financial independence*.

The bottom line is this: You must start now with a sound budget plan and strategy. So congratulate yourself and buckle down for a victorious ride, using this book as the compass and road map to financial independence.

*Simone Atkinson, president and owner of Faith Build Financials Inc. For more information on where to start saving and how to win financially, apply* Strategies You Can Use to Lower Your Taxes, *outpace inflation, and make your money work harder for you, you may contact Simone Atkinson, MBA Finance, at faithbuildfinancials@gmail.com (e-mail) or 754-264-3640 (office) for a free consultation.*

# PREFACE:

## REASON TO CHOOSE THIS BUDGETING WORKBOOK

This budgeting book is a great financial asset that will help it's user to spend their money in a responsible manner and guide them away from spending that can put them in an unmanageable debt.

One of the great benefits of this book is the fact that both single people and couples can use it as a budgeting plan. It will be especially beneficial for a young person who is about to graduate or who has recently graduated from school.

Many people's debt and credit problems begin either while they are in high school or college or shortly after they leave school to begin a constructive and successful future.

This book's purpose is to teach you how to prevent unnecessary spending that will result in unmanageable debt and to expand or begin a savings toward a healthier financial future.

Why a "budget" plan? Because following a budget will guide your spending habits in such a way that encourages you to save rather than spending your money unnecessarily. It is no secret that many (not all) people are in debt all because of their spending patterns. A budget can also prepare you for emergencies and unexpected expenses, both small and large, which otherwise might put you in unmanageable debt and/or just might cause you to lose your possessions.

Where money is a concern, money management can help improve some family and friend relationships and even some marriages as well. You can think of this budget not just as a spending guide, but also as a savings plan.

# GETTING STARTED WITH YOUR BUDGET

## HOW TO USE THIS BOOK

THE first step in starting your budgeting is to write the starting date in the space provided at the upper-right hand corner (see example # 1).

THE second step is to write in all your monthly income in the appropriate place(s) on the budget sheet (see example # 2).

THE third step is to write in the cost of each item that applies to you in the second column to the right of the expenses column. For example: the cost of the car payment should be written in the cell to the right of "Car(s)/vehicle(s) Payment", in the second column which is the "Cost column" with the dollar ("$") symbol (see example # 3).

THE fourth step is to review your budget list, double-checking your selections to ensure that the cost of all your applicable expenditure are written down, and each are in their correct row and column (see example # 3).

After you have recorded all your monthly expenses in their appropriate places, an examination for elimination needs to be done. The reason for this examination is to help you identify unnecessary expenditures. I strongly suggest that you get someone with good money management skills to assist you with this elimination process. Why? Because without assistance, you just might overlook something that might not be necessary or wise for you to be spending money on at that time in your life. In addition, by having someone to assist you with this process, you will be better able to identify and eliminate any unnecessary expenses that may have been the culprit(s) keeping you in debt (if you are in debt), or it will help you avoid getting into unnecessary debt. And by following your budget, you will always be aware of hidden pitfalls.

### What Are Hidden Pitfalls?

Hidden pitfalls are those little purchases that add up to more than you think or expect—especially the cents, which we often times don't lookout for—that, when you add them up, can potentially put you over your *spending limit.*

Following your budget is a good way of knowing how your money is being spent. Budgeting should be done after taxes have been deducted and not before. In other words, your budget should be based on your net income, not your gross.

The next step is to write in the due dates of all your expenses in the "Due Date" column (see example # 4).

Next: When the full amount of a bill is paid, it should be written in the column which reads "Paid" (see example # 5).

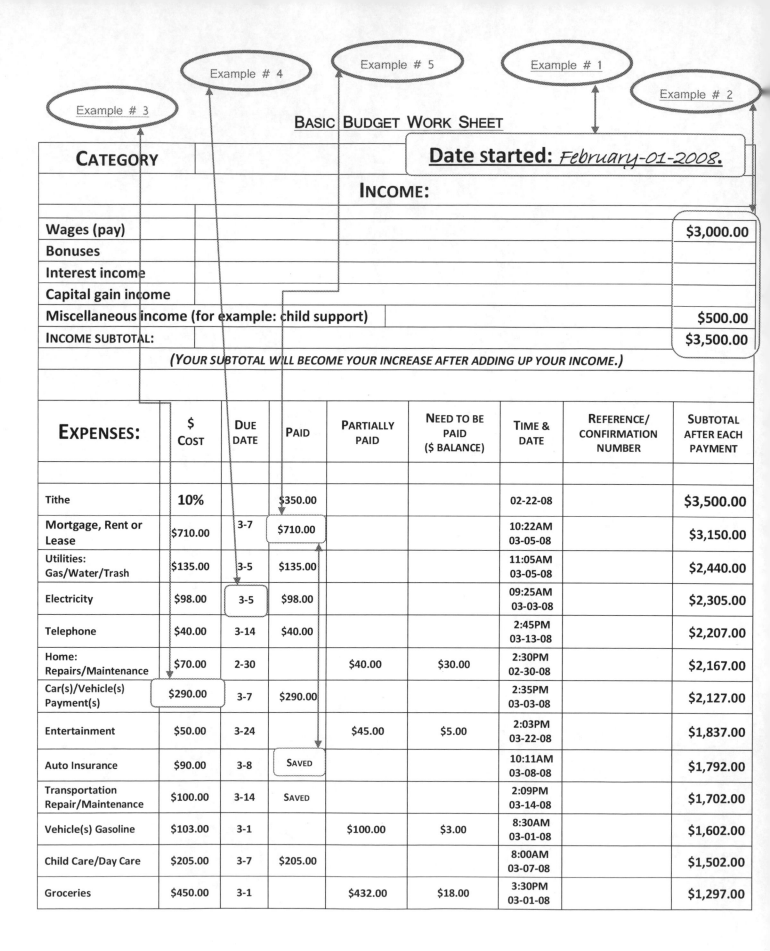

Example # 3

Example # 4

Example # 5

Example # 1

Example # 2

BASIC BUDGET WORK SHEET

| CATEGORY | | Date started: *February-01-2008.* |
|---|---|---|

**INCOME:**

| | |
|---|---|
| Wages (pay) | $3,000.00 |
| Bonuses | |
| Interest income | |
| Capital gain income | |
| Miscellaneous income (for example: child support) | $500.00 |
| INCOME SUBTOTAL: | $3,500.00 |

*(YOUR SUBTOTAL WILL BECOME YOUR INCREASE AFTER ADDING UP YOUR INCOME.)*

| EXPENSES: | $ COST | DUE DATE | PAID | PARTIALLY PAID | NEED TO BE PAID ($ BALANCE) | TIME & DATE | REFERENCE/ CONFIRMATION NUMBER | SUBTOTAL AFTER EACH PAYMENT |
|---|---|---|---|---|---|---|---|---|
| Tithe | 10% | | $350.00 | | | 02-22-08 | | $3,500.00 |
| Mortgage, Rent or Lease | $710.00 | 3-7 | $710.00 | | | 10:22AM 03-05-08 | | $3,150.00 |
| Utilities: Gas/Water/Trash | $135.00 | 3-5 | $135.00 | | | 11:05AM 03-05-08 | | $2,440.00 |
| Electricity | $98.00 | 3-5 | $98.00 | | | 09:25AM 03-03-08 | | $2,305.00 |
| Telephone | $40.00 | 3-14 | $40.00 | | | 2:45PM 03-13-08 | | $2,207.00 |
| Home: Repairs/Maintenance | $70.00 | 2-30 | | $40.00 | $30.00 | 2:30PM 02-30-08 | | $2,167.00 |
| Car(s)/Vehicle(s) Payment(s) | $290.00 | 3-7 | $290.00 | | | 2:35PM 03-03-08 | | $2,127.00 |
| Entertainment | $50.00 | 3-24 | | $45.00 | $5.00 | 2:03PM 03-22-08 | | $1,837.00 |
| Auto Insurance | $90.00 | 3-8 | SAVED | | | 10:11AM 03-08-08 | | $1,792.00 |
| Transportation Repair/Maintenance | $100.00 | 3-14 | SAVED | | | 2:09PM 03-14-08 | | $1,702.00 |
| Vehicle(s) Gasoline | $103.00 | 3-1 | | $100.00 | $3.00 | 8:30AM 03-01-08 | | $1,602.00 |
| Child Care/Day Care | $205.00 | 3-7 | $205.00 | | | 8:00AM 03-07-08 | | $1,502.00 |
| Groceries | $450.00 | 3-1 | | $432.00 | $18.00 | 3:30PM 03-01-08 | | $1,297.00 |

| | | | | | | | | |
|---|---|---|---|---|---|---|---|---|
| Other Transportation: Tolls; Bus; Subway, Etc. | | | | | | | | |
| Toiletries/Household Products | $80.00 | 3-1 | | $67.00 | $13.00 | 3:41PM 03-01-08 | | $865.00 |
| Allowance(s) | $100.00 | 3-3 | $100.00 | | | 8:50AM 03-01-08 | | $798.00 |
| College Tuition | | | | | | | | |
| Clothing | $125.00 | 3-5 | | $107.00 | $18.00 | 5:30PM 03-01-08 | | $698.00 |
| Eating Out | $70.00 | 3-2 | | $35.39 | $34.61 | 7:15PM 03-01-08 | | $591.00 |
| Personal Property Tax | | | | | | | | |
| Pets (Food and Care) | $50.00 | 3-1 | | $42.00 | $8.00 | 3:43PM 03-01-08 | | $555.61 |
| Saving(s) | $137.00 | 3-3 | SAVED | | | 10:05AM 03-03-08 | | $513.61 |
| Hobbies | | | | | | | | |
| Gift(s)/Donation(s) | $40.00 | 3-2 | $40.00 | | | 10:00AM 03-02-08 | | $376.61 |
| Entertainment/Recreation | $57.00 | 3-26 | | $49.52 | $7.48 | 9:30AM 03-22-08 | | $336.61 |
| Credit Card Payment(s) | $55.00 | 3-20 | $55.00 | | | 11:00 AM 03-10-08 | Z5d7qc8sf | $287.09 |
| Health Care | | | | | | | | |
| Emergency | $95.00 | 3-3 | SAVED | | | 10:15AM 03-03-08 | | $232.09 |
| Dental | | | | | | | | |
| Vision | | | | | | | | |
| Miscellaneous Expense | | | | | | | | |
| | | | | | | | | |
| EXPENSES SUBTOTAL: | $2,653.00 | | | | | | | |
| | | | | | | | | |
| CURRENTLY IN SAVING ACCOUNT: | $355.00 | | | | | | | |
| | | | | | | | | |
| REMAIN IN CHECKING ACCOUNT: | | | | | | | | $137.09 |

Example # 6

Example # 7

Example # 8

Example # 9

Example #10

You should not mark a bill as paid until it is paid in full; if you paid part of a bill, write down the amount you paid in the "Partially Paid" column (see example # 6).

Then, write the remainder of that partially paid bill in the "Need to Be Paid ($ Balance)" column, to remind yourself that it needs to be paid (see example # 7). This action will remind you that this bill was not paid in full, just in case you should forget.

For expenses that might occur more than once a year but not every month, divide the expense by the number of months that it occurs and add it to the budgeting list, as if it is due each month. For example, If the auto insurance bill is due every six months, divide it by six and save that amount each month until about ten business days from the appointed due date. *It should be written in your budget book as "saved" in the paid column* (see example # 5). Then, pay the bill about ten business days before the due date in order to ensure that the recipient receives the payment on time.

Record the time and date that you make each payment in the "Time & Date" column (see example # 8) for future references.

The eighth column allows for you to record the reference or confirmation number if one is issued after a payment was made. This will help to provide proof of payment to whomsoever it may concern in the event that a discrepancy concerning a payment should arise (see example # 9).

Deduct each payment made from the amount located in the same row, but in the "Subtotal after Each Payment" column only, and bring the remainder to the next applicable expense row below the previous subtotal (see example #10).

When starting a new sheet, be sure to add any previous balance from the old to the new sheet in order to keep your budget up to date.

This plan will enable you to make wise spending decisions and will provide you with critical balance information for each category at all times.

# WORDS OF WISDOM

# SECRET STRATEGY

If you have a credit card, I have a little *Secret Strategy* that I will share with you. It is a strategy that requires a small amount of discipline. (However, if you're following the "Budget," you're already exercising discipline, so this should really be a breeze). I recommend you use your credit cards to pay all bills that accept credit card payment. First, start with a credit card that is open but has a zero balance. This is crucial. Second, make those payments with that credit card. Third, use the money that you would normally use to pay those bills to pay off the credit card balance in full each month. Don't worry about the interest rate on the card. *Most* credit cards, when paid in full each month, waive any interest for that month. It is when you carry a balance over to the next month that a finance charge will be added to your balance. You can check this with a quick phone call to your credit card company. The customer service phone number can usually be found on the back of the credit card.

Here is why I recommend this strategy: Using credit cards to pay those bills and, in turn, paying off the card's balance with the money you already set aside for those bills will help increase your "FICO SCORE." This is because each month that you pay off that credit card balance, the credit card company reports an "on time" payment to the Credit Bureau. And each month, you will accumulate another "on time" mark. The more accumulated "on time" marks on your credit report, the more your FICO Score is affected positively. Some people do not realize that your payment history with the electric company or your cell phone provider, or your water company is *not* reported to the credit Bureaus (unless you seriously default on any of them and are sent to a collection agency for remaining balances, which does show up on your credit report). So, you guessed it! By not taking advantage of this strategy, you could be making perfect, on time payments for years on some of your bills, but essentially no one (most importantly, the credit bureaus) would know!

A debit or check card from your bank does not offer the benefit of building your credit score, even if it bears the visa or MasterCard logo. Therefore, other than to withdraw cash, why use a debit card if it will not yield you the opportunity of increasing your credit score? My strategy allows you to kill two birds with one stone. You will be actively building a positive credit history and increasing your very important credit score, and keeping those bills paid all at the same time.

# LET YOUR CREDIT WORK IN YOUR FAVOR

It would be more progressive, in terms of the amount of credit *points* earned in a short period of time, if you have each item (expenses or bill, if you will) on its own credit card. For example, you'd have one credit card for the light bill, a separate credit card for the water bill, another card for your auto insurance, and a completely different card for the mortgage. If you have more than one vehicle, each vehicle should be on its own credit card. In other words, only one item should be assigned to a card, for as long as you owe on the item, regardless of the card's credit limit.

Note that it is **VERY IMPORTANT** that you open these accounts with a little extra cash to serve as a *cushion*! For example, even though my car payment was $330.00 a month, I opened a secure credit card account for $355.00 and used that card to make my car payment each month, and I did not use that credit card for anything else. My cushion for that card was $25. The cushion ensures that, if a little more than the $330.00 were to be deducted from the card, the card wouldn't go over its limit. If you are concerned that you may be tempted to use that particular card for something other than what you opened it for, follow what I am about to instruct you to do, and you won't have to worry about misusing it!

**INSTRUCTIONS:**

Step 1: Buy a book with all blank pages—a diary, if you will.

Step 2: Write down the following information on the card in the book: the *name* of the card; the *sixteen-digit number* that appears on the front of the card; the *exact* way in which *your name* appears on the card; the *type* of card (for example, MasterCard); the *expiration* date; the *CVV* (security) number, which is located next to the signature strip on the back of the card (three digits); and all *contact information* associated with the card, including phone number, address, and Web site, if provided. **AFTER YOU HAVE RECORDED THIS INFORMATION, BE SURE TO STORE THE BOOK IN A SECURE PLACE TO PREVENT YOUR PERSONAL INFORMATION FROM BEING STOLEN!**

Step 3: Call the company to whom you owe the debt for which you opened the account and set up automatic monthly payments to be made from that specific secure credit card account. When you call the company to whom you owe the debt, be sure to request that the company takes the payment on a date convenient to you. For example, my car payment was due on the tenth of the month, but I called my financing company and requested that it be withdrawn on the twenty-seventh of each month instead. This allowed me to have two pay periods each month before my car payment was due, which enabled me to ensure that the funds were available on my secured credit card for my car payment to be deducted on time without any problems. Please keep in mind that the money on the secure credit card will be 100 percent yours because it will require your cash to open this kind of account. And even if the credit card was not a "secure credit card," if you follow my instructions, *your credit* will still *work* in *your favor.* The same was possible for me all because I used my car payment, which I already had, to pay for my car by going *through* a credit card company *without using that company's money.* How did I go *through* a credit card company? Answer: I pay off the card in full immediately after my car payment was deducted. Therefore, I never carry over a balance on that card (or any other card that is assigned to a monthly bill) to the following month, *so in terms of fees, it remains as if the card was never used. Yet, at the same time, the card company will report to the credit bureaus each month that you paid it both on time and in full.*

Step 4: After you have done as I instructed above, get a pair of scissors and put them to work on that card. Be sure to set up automatic payment for the item just before you cut that card to pieces and make sure that, as you set up an automatic payment for a debt, you cut that card right away, so that you avoid making the mistake of setting up automatic payment for another bill on the same card!

I know it may seem like a bit of a stretch to do all this, but in the end, you will see that it was worth it all.

In order to get a bill on its own credit card, I strongly recommend that you go to a bank that offers what is known as a "secure credit card" and open a secure credit card for each bill. Please make sure that the bill can be paid with a credit card before you open a secure credit card account for that bill! I would also have you to know that not all banks offer this kind of account. However, I think it is very important for a person who is trying to *build* or *rebuild* their credit to take advantage of this wonderful opportunity.

One of the banks that I had the pleasure of opening this kind of account with is Citibank. After the customer service I've experienced from time to time, I highly recommend the institution. However, if you feel you would rather use another bank, then by all means, do so. My objective here is for you to have your credit working for you.

Before you open your secure credit card account, it is very important to make sure that your chosen bank is insured by the FDIC (**Federal Deposit Insurance Corporation**), in the United States, or an equivalent corporation in your country, if such services are available for its residents! It is absolutely imperative that you bank with an FDIC-insured institution (**or one that is secured by a similar corporation outside of the United States**).

What is the FDIC? **The FDIC is** an independent agency that the US Congress created to maintain stability and public confidence in the US banking system. You can read more about the FDIC by researching "FDIC" on any of several search engines available on the internet.

It is widely believed that having credit cards is a bad thing. Some people don't even have one, for fear of accumulating too much debt. However, contrary to that belief, the opposite is most certainly true. Having one or more credit cards is never a bad thing. It is *how* you use the card that will determine if the card will put you in debt or not. By following this budgeting book, an individual will most certainly shorten the time period it would normally require to build, rebuild, or even achieve good or excellent credit. And that's how you make your credit work for you!

## Factors that Impact Your Credit Score

There are several scoring models used in the marketplace, and each lender has its own set of scoring model factors. The way in which each lender decides their chosen factors may vary from each other. However, the exact method used to calculate your score is proprietary. Basically, the higher your score, the better your chances are of obtaining favorable terms and rates.

## Fixing or Improving Your Credit Score

A person's credit *history* is very important, and maintaining a credit *score* in good standing is very important as well. Therefore, I recommend that you check your credit report frequently to make sure that your score is, and remains in good standing. What many people don't know is that they don't have to pay someone else to fix their credit. That's right. You can fix it yourself. It may seem like too much work, but the truth is, it's not a lot of work. Nor is it difficult to do. When you check your credit report, you will be able to see what, if anything, is negatively affecting your credit score, and you will be able to dispute or set up a payment plan to improve your credit.

I would never recommend that anyone have his or her credit checked by a lender or anyone who, by so doing, can lower the score. This negative impact is the reason why I strongly recommend you check your score yourself, and by checking it yourself, your score will not go down. And doing so is very easy. There are several ways for you to check your own credit report. One, which I have personally used, is freecreditreport.com (http://www.freecreditreport.com). Using this Web Site, I can monitor my credit report and score from all three credit reporting agencies on a daily basis if I choose to, and I receive alert notifications when key changes occur. The internet is not the only route by which you can obtain a copy of your credit report. You can also write to any one, or to all three, of the credit reporting agencies (Experian, Equifax, and TransUnion) and request a copy of your credit report. However, while you do have the option of submitting your request in writing (upon receiving your request, the agency may take anywhere from three to ten business days to respond), for a faster response, I recommend using the internet, where the process is much more expeditious. One of the benefits that I received, and enjoy, from freecreditreport.com is the bi-monthly monitoring of my Experian credit score with alert notification when the score goes up or down, or moves me into a different risk level. Also, I receive unlimited access to my Experian credit report so that I can view it whenever I desire. In fact, freecreditreport.com even gives me a summary of the key financial information that lenders use to rate me, and I'm sure the company will do the same for you.

Why is your credit score so important? Please keep in mind that lenders use your credit scores to help them determine your "credit worthiness" when you are applying for credit cards, loans, or lines of credit. Lending institutions may use your credit score for figuring out whether you qualify for a loan and, if so, what terms and interest rates you will receive.

Another important benefit that freecreditreport.com provides—a benefit I believe you will enjoy as much as I do—is the wonderful option of talking to a live representative when you call the toll free contact number. And even though their business hours may vary from day to day, you can usually reach someone on any day of the week, including weekends. Heaven knows how much I hate dealing with automated answering systems when I call an 800, or business, number, and I may be speaking for you as well. A live representative to whom you can voice your concerns is much more welcoming than dealing with an automated system.

## The Way Your Credit Score is Calculated

Your credit scores are calculated based on information in your credit reports, and as fluid numbers change, sometimes on a daily basis. This is why it is very important for you to stay informed about your credit reports. Being aware of what's going on with them will ensure that you have some (if not all) control of the changes that could affect your credit scores. Other than checking your credit score from time to time, credit monitoring is the best way for you to know what is happening in your credit report.

## Allowance Account

Another great piece of advice, which I recommend not only for a single person or parent, but for couples as well, is an allowance account. It is very important for you to have, and commit yourself to, an allowance each month, in order to promptly achieve a good credit history. More on allowance accounts can be found in my previous book, *In A World Of Darkness, Let There Be Light!*, which is available at various book stores and on the internet. Self-discipline is necessary to acquire a better financial future. Fortunately, you will be able to master this ability once you've implemented this budgeting plan and followed the step-by-step processes outlined in this book. Overall, this budgeting plan will be beneficial for anyone in need of a brighter financial future.

Now that all is said and done, how about we get started on the road to a better financial future?

# BASIC BUDGET WORK SHEETS

# Basic Budget Work Sheet

| CATEGORY | Date Started: |
|---|---|
| **INCOME:** | |
| Wages (pay) | |
| Bonuses | |
| Interest income | |
| Capital gain income | |
| Miscellaneous income (for example: child support) | |
| INCOME SUBTOTAL: | |

*(YOUR SUBTOTAL WILL BECOME YOUR INCREASE AFTER YOU ADD UP YOUR INCOME.)*

| EXPENSES: | $ COST | DUE DATE | PAID | PARTIALLY PAID | NEED TO BE PAID ($ BALANCE) | TIME & DATE | REFERENCE/CON FIRMATION NUMBER | SUBTOTAL AFTER EACH PAYMENT |
|---|---|---|---|---|---|---|---|---|
| | | | | | | | | |
| Tithe | 10% | | | | | | | |
| Mortgage, Rent or Lease | | | | | | | | |
| Utilities: Gas/Water/ Trash | | | | | | | | |
| Electricity | | | | | | | | |
| Telephone | | | | | | | | |
| Home: Repairs/Maintenance | | | | | | | | |
| Car(s)/Vehicle(s) Payment(s) | | | | | | | | |
| Entertainment | | | | | | | | |
| Auto Insurance | | | | | | | | |
| Transportation Maintenance/Repair | | | | | | | | |
| Vehicle(s) Gasoline | | | | | | | | |
| Child Care/Day Care | | | | | | | | |
| Groceries | | | | | | | | |

| | | | | | | | |
|---|---|---|---|---|---|---|---|
| **Other Transportation: Tolls, Bus, Subway, Etc.** | | | | | | | |
| **Toiletries/Household Products** | | | | | | | |
| **Allowance(s)** | | | | | | | |
| **College Tuition** | | | | | | | |
| **Clothing** | | | | | | | |
| **Eating Out** | | | | | | | |
| **Personal Property Tax** | | | | | | | |
| **Pets (Food and Care)** | | | | | | | |
| **Saving(s)** | | | | | | | |
| **Hobbies** | | | | | | | |
| **Gift(s)/Donation(s)** | | | | | | | |
| **Entertainment/Recreation** | | | | | | | |
| **Credit Card Payment(s)** | | | | | | | |
| **Health Care** | | | | | | | |
| **Emergency** | | | | | | | |
| **Dental** | | | | | | | |
| **Vision** | | | | | | | |
| **Miscellaneous Expense** | | | | | | | |
| **Miscellaneous Expense** | | | | | | | |
| **Miscellaneous Expense** | | | | | | | |
| | | | | | | | |
| **EXPENSES SUBTOTAL:** | | | | | | | |
| | | | | | | | |
| **CURRENTLY IN SAVING ACCOUNT:** | | | | | | | |
| | | | | | | | |
| **REMAIN IN CHECKING ACCOUNT:** | | | | | | | |

# BASIC BUDGET WORK SHEET

| CATEGORY | Date Started: |
|---|---|
| **INCOME:** | |
| Wages (pay) | |
| Bonuses | |
| Interest income | |
| Capital gain income | |
| Miscellaneous income (for example: child support) | |
| INCOME SUBTOTAL: | |
| *(YOUR SUBTOTAL WILL BECOME YOUR INCREASE AFTER YOU ADD UP YOUR INCOME.)* | |

| EXPENSES: | $ COST | DUE DATE | PAID | PARTIALLY PAID | NEED TO BE PAID ($ BALANCE) | TIME & DATE | REFERENCE/CON FIRMATION NUMBER | SUBTOTAL AFTER EACH PAYMENT |
|---|---|---|---|---|---|---|---|---|
| | | | | | | | | |
| Tithe | 10% | | | | | | | |
| Mortgage, Rent or Lease | | | | | | | | |
| Utilities: Gas/Water/ Trash | | | | | | | | |
| Electricity | | | | | | | | |
| Telephone | | | | | | | | |
| Home: Repairs/Maintenance | | | | | | | | |
| Car(s)/Vehicle(s) Payment(s) | | | | | | | | |
| Entertainment | | | | | | | | |
| Auto Insurance | | | | | | | | |
| Transportation Maintenance/Repair | | | | | | | | |
| Vehicle(s) Gasoline | | | | | | | | |
| Child Care/Day Care | | | | | | | | |
| Groceries | | | | | | | | |

| | | | | | | | |
|---|---|---|---|---|---|---|---|
| **Other Transportation: Tolls, Bus, Subway, Etc.** | | | | | | | |
| **Toiletries/Household Products** | | | | | | | |
| **Allowance(s)** | | | | | | | |
| **College Tuition** | | | | | | | |
| **Clothing** | | | | | | | |
| **Eating Out** | | | | | | | |
| **Personal Property Tax** | | | | | | | |
| **Pets (Food and Care)** | | | | | | | |
| **Saving(s)** | | | | | | | |
| **Hobbies** | | | | | | | |
| **Gift(s)/Donation(s)** | | | | | | | |
| **Entertainment/Recreation** | | | | | | | |
| **Credit Card Payment(s)** | | | | | | | |
| **Health Care** | | | | | | | |
| **Emergency** | | | | | | | |
| **Dental** | | | | | | | |
| **Vision** | | | | | | | |
| **Miscellaneous Expense** | | | | | | | |
| **Miscellaneous Expense** | | | | | | | |
| **Miscellaneous Expense** | | | | | | | |
| | | | | | | | |
| **EXPENSES SUBTOTAL:** | | | | | | | |
| | | | | | | | |
| **CURRENTLY IN SAVING ACCOUNT:** | | | | | | | |
| | | | | | | | |
| **REMAIN IN CHECKING ACCOUNT:** | | | | | | | |

# Basic Budget Work Sheet

| CATEGORY | Date Started: |
|---|---|
| **INCOME:** | |
| Wages (pay) | |
| Bonuses | |
| Interest income | |
| Capital gain income | |
| Miscellaneous income (for example: child support) | |
| INCOME SUBTOTAL: | |

*(YOUR SUBTOTAL WILL BECOME YOUR INCREASE AFTER YOU ADD UP YOUR INCOME.)*

| EXPENSES: | $ COST | DUE DATE | PAID | PARTIALLY PAID | NEED TO BE PAID ($ BALANCE) | TIME & DATE | REFERENCE/CON FIRMATION NUMBER | SUBTOTAL AFTER EACH PAYMENT |
|---|---|---|---|---|---|---|---|---|
| | | | | | | | | |
| Tithe | 10% | | | | | | | |
| Mortgage, Rent or Lease | | | | | | | | |
| Utilities: Gas/Water/ Trash | | | | | | | | |
| Electricity | | | | | | | | |
| Telephone | | | | | | | | |
| Home: Repairs/Maintenance | | | | | | | | |
| Car(s)/Vehicle(s) Payment(s) | | | | | | | | |
| Entertainment | | | | | | | | |
| Auto Insurance | | | | | | | | |
| Transportation Maintenance/Repair | | | | | | | | |
| Vehicle(s) Gasoline | | | | | | | | |
| Child Care/Day Care | | | | | | | | |
| Groceries | | | | | | | | |

| | | | | | | | | |
|---|---|---|---|---|---|---|---|---|
| **Other Transportation: Tolls, Bus, Subway, Etc.** | | | | | | | | |
| **Toiletries/Household Products** | | | | | | | | |
| **Allowance(s)** | | | | | | | | |
| **College Tuition** | | | | | | | | |
| **Clothing** | | | | | | | | |
| **Eating Out** | | | | | | | | |
| **Personal Property Tax** | | | | | | | | |
| **Pets (Food and Care)** | | | | | | | | |
| **Saving(s)** | | | | | | | | |
| **Hobbies** | | | | | | | | |
| **Gift(s)/Donation(s)** | | | | | | | | |
| **Entertainment/Recreation** | | | | | | | | |
| **Credit Card Payment(s)** | | | | | | | | |
| **Health Care** | | | | | | | | |
| **Emergency** | | | | | | | | |
| **Dental** | | | | | | | | |
| **Vision** | | | | | | | | |
| **Miscellaneous Expense** | | | | | | | | |
| **Miscellaneous Expense** | | | | | | | | |
| **Miscellaneous Expense** | | | | | | | | |
| | | | | | | | | |
| **EXPENSES SUBTOTAL:** | | | | | | | | |
| | | | | | | | | |
| **CURRENTLY IN SAVING ACCOUNT:** | | | | | | | | |
| | | | | | | | | |
| **REMAIN IN CHECKING ACCOUNT:** | | | | | | | | |

# Basic Budget Work Sheet

| CATEGORY | Date Started: |
|---|---|
| INCOME: | |
| Wages (pay) | |
| Bonuses | |
| Interest income | |
| Capital gain income | |
| Miscellaneous income (for example: child support) | |
| INCOME SUBTOTAL: | |
| *(YOUR SUBTOTAL WILL BECOME YOUR INCREASE AFTER YOU ADD UP YOUR INCOME.)* | |

| EXPENSES: | $ COST | DUE DATE | PAID | PARTIALLY PAID | NEED TO BE PAID ($ BALANCE) | TIME & DATE | REFERENCE/CON FIRMATION NUMBER | SUBTOTAL AFTER EACH PAYMENT |
|---|---|---|---|---|---|---|---|---|
| | | | | | | | | |
| Tithe | 10% | | | | | | | |
| Mortgage, Rent or Lease | | | | | | | | |
| Utilities: Gas/Water/ Trash | | | | | | | | |
| Electricity | | | | | | | | |
| Telephone | | | | | | | | |
| Home: Repairs/Maintenance | | | | | | | | |
| Car(s)/Vehicle(s) Payment(s) | | | | | | | | |
| Entertainment | | | | | | | | |
| Auto Insurance | | | | | | | | |
| Transportation Maintenance/Repair | | | | | | | | |
| Vehicle(s) Gasoline | | | | | | | | |
| Child Care/Day Care | | | | | | | | |
| Groceries | | | | | | | | |

| | | | | | | | | |
|---|---|---|---|---|---|---|---|---|
| Other Transportation: Tolls, Bus, Subway, Etc. | | | | | | | | |
| Toiletries/Household Products | | | | | | | | |
| Allowance(s) | | | | | | | | |
| College Tuition | | | | | | | | |
| Clothing | | | | | | | | |
| Eating Out | | | | | | | | |
| Personal Property Tax | | | | | | | | |
| Pets (Food and Care) | | | | | | | | |
| Saving(s) | | | | | | | | |
| Hobbies | | | | | | | | |
| Gift(s)/Donation(s) | | | | | | | | |
| Entertainment/Recreation | | | | | | | | |
| Credit Card Payment(s) | | | | | | | | |
| Health Care | | | | | | | | |
| Emergency | | | | | | | | |
| Dental | | | | | | | | |
| Vision | | | | | | | | |
| Miscellaneous Expense | | | | | | | | |
| Miscellaneous Expense | | | | | | | | |
| Miscellaneous Expense | | | | | | | | |
| | | | | | | | | |
| EXPENSES SUBTOTAL: | | | | | | | | |
| | | | | | | | | |
| CURRENTLY IN SAVING ACCOUNT: | | | | | | | | |
| | | | | | | | | |
| REMAIN IN CHECKING ACCOUNT: | | | | | | | | |

# Basic Budget Work Sheet

| CATEGORY | Date Started: _____ |
|---|---|
| **INCOME:** | |

| | |
|---|---|
| Wages (pay) | |
| Bonuses | |
| Interest income | |
| Capital gain income | |
| Miscellaneous income (for example: child support) | |
| INCOME SUBTOTAL: | |

*(YOUR SUBTOTAL WILL BECOME YOUR INCREASE AFTER YOU ADD UP YOUR INCOME.)*

| EXPENSES: | $ COST | DUE DATE | PAID | PARTIALLY PAID | NEED TO BE PAID ($ BALANCE) | TIME & DATE | REFERENCE/CON FIRMATION NUMBER | SUBTOTAL AFTER EACH PAYMENT |
|---|---|---|---|---|---|---|---|---|
| | | | | | | | | |
| Tithe | 10% | | | | | | | |
| Mortgage, Rent or Lease | | | | | | | | |
| Utilities: Gas/Water/Trash | | | | | | | | |
| Electricity | | | | | | | | |
| Telephone | | | | | | | | |
| Home: Repairs/Maintenance | | | | | | | | |
| Car(s)/Vehicle(s) Payment(s) | | | | | | | | |
| Entertainment | | | | | | | | |
| Auto Insurance | | | | | | | | |
| Transportation Maintenance/Repair | | | | | | | | |
| Vehicle(s) Gasoline | | | | | | | | |
| Child Care/Day Care | | | | | | | | |
| Groceries | | | | | | | | |

| | | | | | | | |
|---|---|---|---|---|---|---|---|
| **Other Transportation: Tolls, Bus, Subway, Etc.** | | | | | | | |
| **Toiletries/Household Products** | | | | | | | |
| **Allowance(s)** | | | | | | | |
| **College Tuition** | | | | | | | |
| **Clothing** | | | | | | | |
| **Eating Out** | | | | | | | |
| **Personal Property Tax** | | | | | | | |
| **Pets (Food and Care)** | | | | | | | |
| **Saving(s)** | | | | | | | |
| **Hobbies** | | | | | | | |
| **Gift(s)/Donation(s)** | | | | | | | |
| **Entertainment/Recreation** | | | | | | | |
| **Credit Card Payment(s)** | | | | | | | |
| **Health Care** | | | | | | | |
| **Emergency** | | | | | | | |
| **Dental** | | | | | | | |
| **Vision** | | | | | | | |
| **Miscellaneous Expense** | | | | | | | |
| **Miscellaneous Expense** | | | | | | | |
| **Miscellaneous Expense** | | | | | | | |
| | | | | | | | |
| **EXPENSES SUBTOTAL:** | | | | | | | |
| | | | | | | | |
| **CURRENTLY IN SAVING ACCOUNT:** | | | | | | | |
| | | | | | | | |
| **REMAIN IN CHECKING ACCOUNT:** | | | | | | | |

# Basic Budget Work Sheet

| CATEGORY | Date Started: |
|----------|---------------|
| **INCOME:** | |

| | |
|---|---|
| Wages (pay) | |
| Bonuses | |
| Interest income | |
| Capital gain income | |
| Miscellaneous income (for example: child support) | |
| INCOME SUBTOTAL: | |

*(YOUR SUBTOTAL WILL BECOME YOUR INCREASE AFTER YOU ADD UP YOUR INCOME.)*

| EXPENSES: | $ COST | DUE DATE | PAID | PARTIALLY PAID | NEED TO BE PAID ($ BALANCE) | TIME & DATE | REFERENCE/CONFIRMATION NUMBER | SUBTOTAL AFTER EACH PAYMENT |
|-----------|--------|----------|------|----------------|-----------------------------|-------------|-------------------------------|------------------------------|
| | | | | | | | | |
| Tithe | 10% | | | | | | | |
| Mortgage, Rent or Lease | | | | | | | | |
| Utilities: Gas/Water/Trash | | | | | | | | |
| Electricity | | | | | | | | |
| Telephone | | | | | | | | |
| Home: Repairs/Maintenance | | | | | | | | |
| Car(s)/Vehicle(s) Payment(s) | | | | | | | | |
| Entertainment | | | | | | | | |
| Auto Insurance | | | | | | | | |
| Transportation Maintenance/Repair | | | | | | | | |
| Vehicle(s) Gasoline | | | | | | | | |
| Child Care/Day Care | | | | | | | | |
| Groceries | | | | | | | | |

| | | | | | | | |
|---|---|---|---|---|---|---|---|
| **Other Transportation: Tolls, Bus, Subway, Etc.** | | | | | | | |
| **Toiletries/Household Products** | | | | | | | |
| **Allowance(s)** | | | | | | | |
| **College Tuition** | | | | | | | |
| **Clothing** | | | | | | | |
| **Eating Out** | | | | | | | |
| **Personal Property Tax** | | | | | | | |
| **Pets (Food and Care)** | | | | | | | |
| **Saving(s)** | | | | | | | |
| **Hobbies** | | | | | | | |
| **Gift(s)/Donation(s)** | | | | | | | |
| **Entertainment/Recreation** | | | | | | | |
| **Credit Card Payment(s)** | | | | | | | |
| **Health Care** | | | | | | | |
| **Emergency** | | | | | | | |
| **Dental** | | | | | | | |
| **Vision** | | | | | | | |
| **Miscellaneous Expense** | | | | | | | |
| **Miscellaneous Expense** | | | | | | | |
| **Miscellaneous Expense** | | | | | | | |
| | | | | | | | |
| **EXPENSES SUBTOTAL:** | | | | | | | |
| | | | | | | | |
| **CURRENTLY IN SAVING ACCOUNT:** | | | | | | | |
| | | | | | | | |
| **REMAIN IN CHECKING ACCOUNT:** | | | | | | | |

# Basic Budget Work Sheet

| CATEGORY | Date Started: |
|---|---|
| **INCOME:** | |
| Wages (pay) | |
| Bonuses | |
| Interest income | |
| Capital gain income | |
| Miscellaneous income (for example: child support) | |
| INCOME SUBTOTAL: | |
| *(YOUR SUBTOTAL WILL BECOME YOUR INCREASE AFTER YOU ADD UP YOUR INCOME.)* | |

| EXPENSES: | $ COST | DUE DATE | PAID | PARTIALLY PAID | NEED TO BE PAID ($ BALANCE) | TIME & DATE | REFERENCE/CON FIRMATION NUMBER | SUBTOTAL AFTER EACH PAYMENT |
|---|---|---|---|---|---|---|---|---|
| | | | | | | | | |
| Tithe | 10% | | | | | | | |
| Mortgage, Rent or Lease | | | | | | | | |
| Utilities: Gas/Water/ Trash | | | | | | | | |
| Electricity | | | | | | | | |
| Telephone | | | | | | | | |
| Home: Repairs/Maintenance | | | | | | | | |
| Car(s)/Vehicle(s) Payment(s) | | | | | | | | |
| Entertainment | | | | | | | | |
| Auto Insurance | | | | | | | | |
| Transportation Maintenance/Repair | | | | | | | | |
| Vehicle(s) Gasoline | | | | | | | | |
| Child Care/Day Care | | | | | | | | |
| Groceries | | | | | | | | |

| | | | | | | | | |
|---|---|---|---|---|---|---|---|---|
| **Other Transportation: Tolls, Bus, Subway, Etc.** | | | | | | | | |
| **Toiletries/Household Products** | | | | | | | | |
| **Allowance(s)** | | | | | | | | |
| **College Tuition** | | | | | | | | |
| **Clothing** | | | | | | | | |
| **Eating Out** | | | | | | | | |
| **Personal Property Tax** | | | | | | | | |
| **Pets (Food and Care)** | | | | | | | | |
| **Saving(s)** | | | | | | | | |
| **Hobbies** | | | | | | | | |
| **Gift(s)/Donation(s)** | | | | | | | | |
| **Entertainment/Recreation** | | | | | | | | |
| **Credit Card Payment(s)** | | | | | | | | |
| **Health Care** | | | | | | | | |
| **Emergency** | | | | | | | | |
| **Dental** | | | | | | | | |
| **Vision** | | | | | | | | |
| **Miscellaneous Expense** | | | | | | | | |
| **Miscellaneous Expense** | | | | | | | | |
| **Miscellaneous Expense** | | | | | | | | |
| | | | | | | | | |
| **EXPENSES SUBTOTAL:** | | | | | | | | |
| | | | | | | | | |
| **CURRENTLY IN SAVING ACCOUNT:** | | | | | | | | |
| | | | | | | | | |
| **REMAIN IN CHECKING ACCOUNT:** | | | | | | | | |

# BASIC BUDGET WORK SHEET

| CATEGORY | Date Started: |
|---|---|
| **INCOME:** | |
| Wages (pay) | |
| Bonuses | |
| Interest income | |
| Capital gain income | |
| Miscellaneous income (for example: child support) | |
| INCOME SUBTOTAL: | |

*(YOUR SUBTOTAL WILL BECOME YOUR INCREASE AFTER YOU ADD UP YOUR INCOME.)*

| EXPENSES: | $ COST | DUE DATE | PAID | PARTIALLY PAID | NEED TO BE PAID ($ BALANCE) | TIME & DATE | REFERENCE/CON FIRMATION NUMBER | SUBTOTAL AFTER EACH PAYMENT |
|---|---|---|---|---|---|---|---|---|
| | | | | | | | | |
| Tithe | 10% | | | | | | | |
| Mortgage, Rent or Lease | | | | | | | | |
| Utilities: Gas/Water/ Trash | | | | | | | | |
| Electricity | | | | | | | | |
| Telephone | | | | | | | | |
| Home: Repairs/Maintenance | | | | | | | | |
| Car(s)/Vehicle(s) Payment(s) | | | | | | | | |
| Entertainment | | | | | | | | |
| Auto Insurance | | | | | | | | |
| Transportation Maintenance/Repair | | | | | | | | |
| Vehicle(s) Gasoline | | | | | | | | |
| Child Care/Day Care | | | | | | | | |
| Groceries | | | | | | | | |

| | | | | | | | |
|---|---|---|---|---|---|---|---|
| **Other Transportation: Tolls, Bus, Subway, Etc.** | | | | | | | |
| **Toiletries/Household Products** | | | | | | | |
| **Allowance(s)** | | | | | | | |
| **College Tuition** | | | | | | | |
| **Clothing** | | | | | | | |
| **Eating Out** | | | | | | | |
| **Personal Property Tax** | | | | | | | |
| **Pets (Food and Care)** | | | | | | | |
| **Saving(s)** | | | | | | | |
| **Hobbies** | | | | | | | |
| **Gift(s)/Donation(s)** | | | | | | | |
| **Entertainment/Recreation** | | | | | | | |
| **Credit Card Payment(s)** | | | | | | | |
| **Health Care** | | | | | | | |
| **Emergency** | | | | | | | |
| **Dental** | | | | | | | |
| **Vision** | | | | | | | |
| **Miscellaneous Expense** | | | | | | | |
| **Miscellaneous Expense** | | | | | | | |
| **Miscellaneous Expense** | | | | | | | |
| | | | | | | | |
| **EXPENSES SUBTOTAL:** | | | | | | | |
| | | | | | | | |
| **CURRENTLY IN SAVING ACCOUNT:** | | | | | | | |
| | | | | | | | |
| **REMAIN IN CHECKING ACCOUNT:** | | | | | | | |

# BASIC BUDGET WORK SHEET

| CATEGORY | Date Started: |
|---|---|
| **INCOME:** | |
| Wages (pay) | |
| Bonuses | |
| Interest income | |
| Capital gain income | |
| Miscellaneous income (for example: child support) | |
| INCOME SUBTOTAL: | |
| *(YOUR SUBTOTAL WILL BECOME YOUR INCREASE AFTER YOU ADD UP YOUR INCOME.)* | |

| EXPENSES: | $ COST | DUE DATE | PAID | PARTIALLY PAID | NEED TO BE PAID ($ BALANCE) | TIME & DATE | REFERENCE/CON FIRMATION NUMBER | SUBTOTAL AFTER EACH PAYMENT |
|---|---|---|---|---|---|---|---|---|
| | | | | | | | | |
| Tithe | 10% | | | | | | | |
| Mortgage, Rent or Lease | | | | | | | | |
| Utilities: Gas/Water/ Trash | | | | | | | | |
| Electricity | | | | | | | | |
| Telephone | | | | | | | | |
| Home: Repairs/Maintenance | | | | | | | | |
| Car(s)/Vehicle(s) Payment(s) | | | | | | | | |
| Entertainment | | | | | | | | |
| Auto Insurance | | | | | | | | |
| Transportation Maintenance/Repair | | | | | | | | |
| Vehicle(s) Gasoline | | | | | | | | |
| Child Care/Day Care | | | | | | | | |
| Groceries | | | | | | | | |

| | | | | | | | |
|---|---|---|---|---|---|---|---|
| **Other Transportation: Tolls, Bus, Subway, Etc.** | | | | | | | |
| **Toiletries/Household Products** | | | | | | | |
| **Allowance(s)** | | | | | | | |
| **College Tuition** | | | | | | | |
| **Clothing** | | | | | | | |
| **Eating Out** | | | | | | | |
| **Personal Property Tax** | | | | | | | |
| **Pets (Food and Care)** | | | | | | | |
| **Saving(s)** | | | | | | | |
| **Hobbies** | | | | | | | |
| **Gift(s)/Donation(s)** | | | | | | | |
| **Entertainment/Recreation** | | | | | | | |
| **Credit Card Payment(s)** | | | | | | | |
| **Health Care** | | | | | | | |
| **Emergency** | | | | | | | |
| **Dental** | | | | | | | |
| **Vision** | | | | | | | |
| **Miscellaneous Expense** | | | | | | | |
| **Miscellaneous Expense** | | | | | | | |
| **Miscellaneous Expense** | | | | | | | |
| | | | | | | | |
| **EXPENSES SUBTOTAL:** | | | | | | | |
| | | | | | | | |
| **CURRENTLY IN SAVING ACCOUNT:** | | | | | | | |
| | | | | | | | |
| **REMAIN IN CHECKING ACCOUNT:** | | | | | | | |

# Basic Budget Work Sheet

| Category | Date Started: |
|---|---|
| **INCOME:** | |
| Wages (pay) | |
| Bonuses | |
| Interest income | |
| Capital gain income | |
| Miscellaneous income (for example: child support) | |
| INCOME SUBTOTAL: | |

*(YOUR SUBTOTAL WILL BECOME YOUR INCREASE AFTER YOU ADD UP YOUR INCOME.)*

| EXPENSES: | $ COST | DUE DATE | PAID | PARTIALLY PAID | NEED TO BE PAID ($ BALANCE) | TIME & DATE | REFERENCE/CON FIRMATION NUMBER | SUBTOTAL AFTER EACH PAYMENT |
|---|---|---|---|---|---|---|---|---|
| | | | | | | | | |
| Tithe | 10% | | | | | | | |
| Mortgage, Rent or Lease | | | | | | | | |
| Utilities: Gas/Water/ Trash | | | | | | | | |
| Electricity | | | | | | | | |
| Telephone | | | | | | | | |
| Home: Repairs/Maintenance | | | | | | | | |
| Car(s)/Vehicle(s) Payment(s) | | | | | | | | |
| Entertainment | | | | | | | | |
| Auto Insurance | | | | | | | | |
| Transportation Maintenance/Repair | | | | | | | | |
| Vehicle(s) Gasoline | | | | | | | | |
| Child Care/Day Care | | | | | | | | |
| Groceries | | | | | | | | |

| | | | | | | | |
|---|---|---|---|---|---|---|---|
| **Other Transportation: Tolls, Bus, Subway, Etc.** | | | | | | | |
| **Toiletries/Household Products** | | | | | | | |
| **Allowance(s)** | | | | | | | |
| **College Tuition** | | | | | | | |
| **Clothing** | | | | | | | |
| **Eating Out** | | | | | | | |
| **Personal Property Tax** | | | | | | | |
| **Pets (Food and Care)** | | | | | | | |
| **Saving(s)** | | | | | | | |
| **Hobbies** | | | | | | | |
| **Gift(s)/Donation(s)** | | | | | | | |
| **Entertainment/Recreation** | | | | | | | |
| **Credit Card Payment(s)** | | | | | | | |
| **Health Care** | | | | | | | |
| **Emergency** | | | | | | | |
| **Dental** | | | | | | | |
| **Vision** | | | | | | | |
| **Miscellaneous Expense** | | | | | | | |
| **Miscellaneous Expense** | | | | | | | |
| **Miscellaneous Expense** | | | | | | | |
| | | | | | | | |
| **EXPENSES SUBTOTAL:** | | | | | | | |
| | | | | | | | |
| **CURRENTLY IN SAVING ACCOUNT:** | | | | | | | |
| | | | | | | | |
| **REMAIN IN CHECKING ACCOUNT:** | | | | | | | |

# BASIC BUDGET WORK SHEET

| CATEGORY | Date Started: |
|---|---|
| **INCOME:** | |
| Wages (pay) | |
| Bonuses | |
| Interest income | |
| Capital gain income | |
| Miscellaneous income (for example: child support) | |
| INCOME SUBTOTAL: | |

*(YOUR SUBTOTAL WILL BECOME YOUR INCREASE AFTER YOU ADD UP YOUR INCOME.)*

| EXPENSES: | $ COST | DUE DATE | PAID | PARTIALLY PAID | NEED TO BE PAID ($ BALANCE) | TIME & DATE | REFERENCE/CON FIRMATION NUMBER | SUBTOTAL AFTER EACH PAYMENT |
|---|---|---|---|---|---|---|---|---|
| | | | | | | | | |
| Tithe | 10% | | | | | | | |
| Mortgage, Rent or Lease | | | | | | | | |
| Utilities: Gas/Water/Trash | | | | | | | | |
| Electricity | | | | | | | | |
| Telephone | | | | | | | | |
| Home: Repairs/Maintenance | | | | | | | | |
| Car(s)/Vehicle(s) Payment(s) | | | | | | | | |
| Entertainment | | | | | | | | |
| Auto Insurance | | | | | | | | |
| Transportation Maintenance/Repair | | | | | | | | |
| Vehicle(s) Gasoline | | | | | | | | |
| Child Care/Day Care | | | | | | | | |
| Groceries | | | | | | | | |

| | | | | | | | | |
|---|---|---|---|---|---|---|---|---|
| **Other Transportation: Tolls, Bus, Subway, Etc.** | | | | | | | | |
| **Toiletries/Household Products** | | | | | | | | |
| **Allowance(s)** | | | | | | | | |
| **College Tuition** | | | | | | | | |
| **Clothing** | | | | | | | | |
| **Eating Out** | | | | | | | | |
| **Personal Property Tax** | | | | | | | | |
| **Pets (Food and Care)** | | | | | | | | |
| **Saving(s)** | | | | | | | | |
| **Hobbies** | | | | | | | | |
| **Gift(s)/Donation(s)** | | | | | | | | |
| **Entertainment/Recreation** | | | | | | | | |
| **Credit Card Payment(s)** | | | | | | | | |
| **Health Care** | | | | | | | | |
| **Emergency** | | | | | | | | |
| **Dental** | | | | | | | | |
| **Vision** | | | | | | | | |
| **Miscellaneous Expense** | | | | | | | | |
| **Miscellaneous Expense** | | | | | | | | |
| **Miscellaneous Expense** | | | | | | | | |
| | | | | | | | | |
| **EXPENSES SUBTOTAL:** | | | | | | | | |
| | | | | | | | | |
| **CURRENTLY IN SAVING ACCOUNT:** | | | | | | | | |
| | | | | | | | | |
| **REMAIN IN CHECKING ACCOUNT:** | | | | | | | | |

# Basic Budget Work Sheet

| CATEGORY | Date Started: _____ |
|---|---|
| **INCOME:** | |
| Wages (pay) | |
| Bonuses | |
| Interest income | |
| Capital gain income | |
| Miscellaneous income (for example: child support) | |
| INCOME SUBTOTAL: | |

*(YOUR SUBTOTAL WILL BECOME YOUR INCREASE AFTER YOU ADD UP YOUR INCOME.)*

| EXPENSES: | $ COST | DUE DATE | PAID | PARTIALLY PAID | NEED TO BE PAID ($ BALANCE) | TIME & DATE | REFERENCE/CONFIRMATION NUMBER | SUBTOTAL AFTER EACH PAYMENT |
|---|---|---|---|---|---|---|---|---|
| | | | | | | | | |
| Tithe | 10% | | | | | | | |
| Mortgage, Rent or Lease | | | | | | | | |
| Utilities: Gas/Water/Trash | | | | | | | | |
| Electricity | | | | | | | | |
| Telephone | | | | | | | | |
| Home: Repairs/Maintenance | | | | | | | | |
| Car(s)/Vehicle(s) Payment(s) | | | | | | | | |
| Entertainment | | | | | | | | |
| Auto Insurance | | | | | | | | |
| Transportation Maintenance/Repair | | | | | | | | |
| Vehicle(s) Gasoline | | | | | | | | |
| Child Care/Day Care | | | | | | | | |
| Groceries | | | | | | | | |

| | | | | | | | | |
|---|---|---|---|---|---|---|---|---|
| **Other Transportation: Tolls, Bus, Subway, Etc.** | | | | | | | | |
| **Toiletries/Household Products** | | | | | | | | |
| **Allowance(s)** | | | | | | | | |
| **College Tuition** | | | | | | | | |
| **Clothing** | | | | | | | | |
| **Eating Out** | | | | | | | | |
| **Personal Property Tax** | | | | | | | | |
| **Pets (Food and Care)** | | | | | | | | |
| **Saving(s)** | | | | | | | | |
| **Hobbies** | | | | | | | | |
| **Gift(s)/Donation(s)** | | | | | | | | |
| **Entertainment/Recreation** | | | | | | | | |
| **Credit Card Payment(s)** | | | | | | | | |
| **Health Care** | | | | | | | | |
| **Emergency** | | | | | | | | |
| **Dental** | | | | | | | | |
| **Vision** | | | | | | | | |
| **Miscellaneous Expense** | | | | | | | | |
| **Miscellaneous Expense** | | | | | | | | |
| **Miscellaneous Expense** | | | | | | | | |
| | | | | | | | | |
| **EXPENSES SUBTOTAL:** | | | | | | | | |
| | | | | | | | | |
| **CURRENTLY IN SAVING ACCOUNT:** | | | | | | | | |
| | | | | | | | | |
| **REMAIN IN CHECKING ACCOUNT:** | | | | | | | | |

# Basic Budget Work Sheet

| CATEGORY | Date Started: |
|---|---|
| **INCOME:** | |
| Wages (pay) | |
| Bonuses | |
| Interest income | |
| Capital gain income | |
| Miscellaneous income (for example: child support) | |
| INCOME SUBTOTAL: | |
| *(YOUR SUBTOTAL WILL BECOME YOUR INCREASE AFTER YOU ADD UP YOUR INCOME.)* | |

| EXPENSES: | $ COST | DUE DATE | PAID | PARTIALLY PAID | NEED TO BE PAID ($ BALANCE) | TIME & DATE | REFERENCE/CON FIRMATION NUMBER | SUBTOTAL AFTER EACH PAYMENT |
|---|---|---|---|---|---|---|---|---|
| | | | | | | | | |
| Tithe | 10% | | | | | | | |
| Mortgage, Rent or Lease | | | | | | | | |
| Utilities: Gas/Water/ Trash | | | | | | | | |
| Electricity | | | | | | | | |
| Telephone | | | | | | | | |
| Home: Repairs/Maintenance | | | | | | | | |
| Car(s)/Vehicle(s) Payment(s) | | | | | | | | |
| Entertainment | | | | | | | | |
| Auto Insurance | | | | | | | | |
| Transportation Maintenance/Repair | | | | | | | | |
| Vehicle(s) Gasoline | | | | | | | | |
| Child Care/Day Care | | | | | | | | |
| Groceries | | | | | | | | |

| | | | | | | | |
|---|---|---|---|---|---|---|---|
| Other Transportation: Tolls, Bus, Subway, Etc. | | | | | | | |
| Toiletries/Household Products | | | | | | | |
| Allowance(s) | | | | | | | |
| College Tuition | | | | | | | |
| Clothing | | | | | | | |
| Eating Out | | | | | | | |
| Personal Property Tax | | | | | | | |
| Pets (Food and Care) | | | | | | | |
| Saving(s) | | | | | | | |
| Hobbies | | | | | | | |
| Gift(s)/Donation(s) | | | | | | | |
| Entertainment/Recreation | | | | | | | |
| Credit Card Payment(s) | | | | | | | |
| Health Care | | | | | | | |
| Emergency | | | | | | | |
| Dental | | | | | | | |
| Vision | | | | | | | |
| Miscellaneous Expense | | | | | | | |
| Miscellaneous Expense | | | | | | | |
| Miscellaneous Expense | | | | | | | |
| | | | | | | | |
| EXPENSES SUBTOTAL: | | | | | | | |
| | | | | | | | |
| CURRENTLY IN SAVING ACCOUNT: | | | | | | | |
| | | | | | | | |
| REMAIN IN CHECKING ACCOUNT: | | | | | | | |

# BASIC BUDGET WORK SHEET

| CATEGORY | Date Started: |
|---|---|

| INCOME: | |
|---|---|
| Wages (pay) | |
| Bonuses | |
| Interest income | |
| Capital gain income | |
| Miscellaneous income (for example: child support) | |
| INCOME SUBTOTAL: | |

*(YOUR SUBTOTAL WILL BECOME YOUR INCREASE AFTER YOU ADD UP YOUR INCOME.)*

| EXPENSES: | $ COST | DUE DATE | PAID | PARTIALLY PAID | NEED TO BE PAID ($ BALANCE) | TIME & DATE | REFERENCE/CON FIRMATION NUMBER | SUBTOTAL AFTER EACH PAYMENT |
|---|---|---|---|---|---|---|---|---|
| | | | | | | | | |
| Tithe | 10% | | | | | | | |
| Mortgage, Rent or Lease | | | | | | | | |
| Utilities: Gas/Water/ Trash | | | | | | | | |
| Electricity | | | | | | | | |
| Telephone | | | | | | | | |
| Home: Repairs/Maintenance | | | | | | | | |
| Car(s)/Vehicle(s) Payment(s) | | | | | | | | . |
| Entertainment | | | | | | | | |
| Auto Insurance | | | | | | | | |
| Transportation Maintenance/Repair | | | | | | | | |
| Vehicle(s) Gasoline | | | | | | | | |
| Child Care/Day Care | | | | | | | | |
| Groceries | | | | | | | | |

| | | | | | | | |
|---|---|---|---|---|---|---|---|
| **Other Transportation: Tolls, Bus, Subway, Etc.** | | | | | | | |
| **Toiletries/Household Products** | | | | | | | |
| **Allowance(s)** | | | | | | | |
| **College Tuition** | | | | | | | |
| **Clothing** | | | | | | | |
| **Eating Out** | | | | | | | |
| **Personal Property Tax** | | | | | | | |
| **Pets (Food and Care)** | | | | | | | |
| **Saving(s)** | | | | | | | |
| **Hobbies** | | | | | | | |
| **Gift(s)/Donation(s)** | | | | | | | |
| **Entertainment/Recreation** | | | | | | | |
| **Credit Card Payment(s)** | | | | | | | |
| **Health Care** | | | | | | | |
| **Emergency** | | | | | | | |
| **Dental** | | | | | | | |
| **Vision** | | | | | | | |
| **Miscellaneous Expense** | | | | | | | |
| **Miscellaneous Expense** | | | | | | | |
| **Miscellaneous Expense** | | | | | | | |
| | | | | | | | |
| **EXPENSES SUBTOTAL:** | | | | | | | |
| | | | | | | | |
| **CURRENTLY IN SAVING ACCOUNT:** | | | | | | | |
| | | | | | | | |
| **REMAIN IN CHECKING ACCOUNT:** | | | | | | | |

# Basic Budget Work Sheet

| Category | Date Started: | | | | | | |
|---|---|---|---|---|---|---|---|
| | **Income:** | | | | | | |
| Wages (pay) | | | | | | | |
| Bonuses | | | | | | | |
| Interest income | | | | | | | |
| Capital gain income | | | | | | | |
| Miscellaneous income (for example: child support) | | | | | | | |
| Income Subtotal: | | | | | | | |
| *(Your subtotal will become your increase after you add up your income.)* | | | | | | | |

| Expenses: | $ Cost | Due Date | Paid | Partially Paid | Need to be Paid ($ Balance) | Time & Date | Reference/Confirmation Number | Subtotal After Each Payment |
|---|---|---|---|---|---|---|---|---|
| | | | | | | | | |
| Tithe | 10% | | | | | | | |
| Mortgage, Rent or Lease | | | | | | | | |
| Utilities: Gas/Water/ Trash | | | | | | | | |
| Electricity | | | | | | | | |
| Telephone | | | | | | | | |
| Home: Repairs/Maintenance | | | | | | | | |
| Car(s)/Vehicle(s) Payment(s) | | | | | | | | |
| Entertainment | | | | | | | | |
| Auto Insurance | | | | | | | | |
| Transportation Maintenance/Repair | | | | | | | | |
| Vehicle(s) Gasoline | | | | | | | | |
| Child Care/Day Care | | | | | | | | |
| Groceries | | | | | | | | |

| | | | | | | | |
|---|---|---|---|---|---|---|---|
| Other Transportation: Tolls, Bus, Subway, Etc. | | | | | | | |
| Toiletries/Household Products | | | | | | | |
| Allowance(s) | | | | | | | |
| College Tuition | | | | | | | |
| Clothing | | | | | | | |
| Eating Out | | | | | | | |
| Personal Property Tax | | | | | | | |
| Pets (Food and Care) | | | | | | | |
| Saving(s) | | | | | | | |
| Hobbies | | | | | | | |
| Gift(s)/Donation(s) | | | | | | | |
| Entertainment/Recreation | | | | | | | |
| Credit Card Payment(s) | | | | | | | |
| Health Care | | | | | | | |
| Emergency | | | | | | | |
| Dental | | | | | | | |
| Vision | | | | | | | |
| Miscellaneous Expense | | | | | | | |
| Miscellaneous Expense | | | | | | | |
| Miscellaneous Expense | | | | | | | |
| | | | | | | | |
| EXPENSES SUBTOTAL: | | | | | | | |
| | | | | | | | |
| CURRENTLY IN SAVING ACCOUNT: | | | | | | | |
| | | | | | | | |
| REMAIN IN CHECKING ACCOUNT: | | | | | | | |

# Basic Budget Work Sheet

| CATEGORY | Date Started: _____ |
|---|---|
| | **INCOME:** |
| Wages (pay) | |
| Bonuses | |
| Interest income | |
| Capital gain income | |
| Miscellaneous income (for example: child support) | |
| INCOME SUBTOTAL: | |
| | *(YOUR SUBTOTAL WILL BECOME YOUR INCREASE AFTER YOU ADD UP YOUR INCOME.)* |

| EXPENSES: | $ COST | DUE DATE | PAID | PARTIALLY PAID | NEED TO BE PAID ($ BALANCE) | TIME & DATE | REFERENCE/CONFIRMATION NUMBER | SUBTOTAL AFTER EACH PAYMENT |
|---|---|---|---|---|---|---|---|---|
| | | | | | | | | |
| Tithe | 10% | | | | | | | |
| Mortgage, Rent or Lease | | | | | | | | |
| Utilities: Gas/Water/Trash | | | | | | | | |
| Electricity | | | | | | | | |
| Telephone | | | | | | | | |
| Home: Repairs/Maintenance | | | | | | | | |
| Car(s)/Vehicle(s) Payment(s) | | | | | | | | |
| Entertainment | | | | | | | | |
| Auto Insurance | | | | | | | | |
| Transportation Maintenance/Repair | | | | | | | | |
| Vehicle(s) Gasoline | | | | | | | | |
| Child Care/Day Care | | | | | | | | |
| Groceries | | | | | | | | |

| | | | | | | | | |
|---|---|---|---|---|---|---|---|---|
| **Other Transportation: Tolls, Bus, Subway, Etc.** | | | | | | | | |
| **Toiletries/Household Products** | | | | | | | | |
| **Allowance(s)** | | | | | | | | |
| **College Tuition** | | | | | | | | |
| **Clothing** | | | | | | | | |
| **Eating Out** | | | | | | | | |
| **Personal Property Tax** | | | | | | | | |
| **Pets (Food and Care)** | | | | | | | | |
| **Saving(s)** | | | | | | | | |
| **Hobbies** | | | | | | | | |
| **Gift(s)/Donation(s)** | | | | | | | | |
| **Entertainment/Recreation** | | | | | | | | |
| **Credit Card Payment(s)** | | | | | | | | |
| **Health Care** | | | | | | | | |
| **Emergency** | | | | | | | | |
| **Dental** | | | | | | | | |
| **Vision** | | | | | | | | |
| **Miscellaneous Expense** | | | | | | | | |
| **Miscellaneous Expense** | | | | | | | | |
| **Miscellaneous Expense** | | | | | | | | |
| | | | | | | | | |
| **EXPENSES SUBTOTAL:** | | | | | | | | |
| | | | | | | | | |
| **CURRENTLY IN SAVING ACCOUNT:** | | | | | | | | |
| | | | | | | | | |
| **REMAIN IN CHECKING ACCOUNT:** | | | | | | | | |

# BASIC BUDGET WORK SHEET

| CATEGORY | Date Started: |
|---|---|
| INCOME: | |
| Wages (pay) | |
| Bonuses | |
| Interest income | |
| Capital gain income | |
| Miscellaneous income (for example: child support) | |
| INCOME SUBTOTAL: | |

*(YOUR SUBTOTAL WILL BECOME YOUR INCREASE AFTER YOU ADD UP YOUR INCOME.)*

| EXPENSES: | $ COST | DUE DATE | PAID | PARTIALLY PAID | NEED TO BE PAID ($ BALANCE) | TIME & DATE | REFERENCE/CONFIRMATION NUMBER | SUBTOTAL AFTER EACH PAYMENT |
|---|---|---|---|---|---|---|---|---|
| | | | | | | | | |
| Tithe | 10% | | | | | | | |
| Mortgage, Rent or Lease | | | | | | | | |
| Utilities: Gas/Water/ Trash | | | | | | | | |
| Electricity | | | | | | | | |
| Telephone | | | | | | | | |
| Home: Repairs/Maintenance | | | | | | | | |
| Car(s)/Vehicle(s) Payment(s) | | | | | | | | |
| Entertainment | | | | | | | | |
| Auto Insurance | | | | | | | | |
| Transportation Maintenance/Repair | | | | | | | | |
| Vehicle(s) Gasoline | | | | | | | | |
| Child Care/Day Care | | | | | | | | |
| Groceries | | | | | | | | |

| | | | | | | | |
|---|---|---|---|---|---|---|---|
| **Other Transportation: Tolls, Bus, Subway, Etc.** | | | | | | | |
| **Toiletries/Household Products** | | | | | | | |
| **Allowance(s)** | | | | | | | |
| **College Tuition** | | | | | | | |
| **Clothing** | | | | | | | |
| **Eating Out** | | | | | | | |
| **Personal Property Tax** | | | | | | | |
| **Pets (Food and Care)** | | | | | | | |
| **Saving(s)** | | | | | | | |
| **Hobbies** | | | | | | | |
| **Gift(s)/Donation(s)** | | | | | | | |
| **Entertainment/Recreation** | | | | | | | |
| **Credit Card Payment(s)** | | | | | | | |
| **Health Care** | | | | | | | |
| **Emergency** | | | | | | | |
| **Dental** | | | | | | | |
| **Vision** | | | | | | | |
| **Miscellaneous Expense** | | | | | | | |
| **Miscellaneous Expense** | | | | | | | |
| **Miscellaneous Expense** | | | | | | | |
| | | | | | | | |
| **EXPENSES SUBTOTAL:** | | | | | | | |
| | | | | | | | |
| **CURRENTLY IN SAVING ACCOUNT:** | | | | | | | |
| | | | | | | | |
| **REMAIN IN CHECKING ACCOUNT:** | | | | | | | |

# Basic Budget Work Sheet

| CATEGORY | Date Started: |
|---|---|
| **INCOME:** | |

| | |
|---|---|
| Wages (pay) | |
| Bonuses | |
| Interest income | |
| Capital gain income | |
| Miscellaneous income (for example: child support) | |
| INCOME SUBTOTAL: | |

*(YOUR SUBTOTAL WILL BECOME YOUR INCREASE AFTER YOU ADD UP YOUR INCOME.)*

| EXPENSES: | $ COST | DUE DATE | PAID | PARTIALLY PAID | NEED TO BE PAID ($ BALANCE) | TIME & DATE | REFERENCE/CON FIRMATION NUMBER | SUBTOTAL AFTER EACH PAYMENT |
|---|---|---|---|---|---|---|---|---|
| | | | | | | | | |
| Tithe | 10% | | | | | | | |
| Mortgage, Rent or Lease | | | | | | | | |
| Utilities: Gas/Water/ Trash | | | | | | | | |
| Electricity | | | | | | | | |
| Telephone | | | | | | | | |
| Home: Repairs/Maintenance | | | | | | | | |
| Car(s)/Vehicle(s) Payment(s) | | | | | | | | |
| Entertainment | | | | | | | | |
| Auto Insurance | | | | | | | | |
| Transportation Maintenance/Repair | | | | | | | | |
| Vehicle(s) Gasoline | | | | | | | | |
| Child Care/Day Care | | | | | | | | |
| Groceries | | | | | | | | |

| | | | | | | | | |
|---|---|---|---|---|---|---|---|---|
| **Other Transportation: Tolls, Bus, Subway, Etc.** | | | | | | | | |
| **Toiletries/Household Products** | | | | | | | | |
| **Allowance(s)** | | | | | | | | |
| **College Tuition** | | | | | | | | |
| **Clothing** | | | | | | | | |
| **Eating Out** | | | | | | | | |
| **Personal Property Tax** | | | | | | | | |
| **Pets (Food and Care)** | | | | | | | | |
| **Saving(s)** | | | | | | | | |
| **Hobbies** | | | | | | | | |
| **Gift(s)/Donation(s)** | | | | | | | | |
| **Entertainment/Recreation** | | | | | | | | |
| **Credit Card Payment(s)** | | | | | | | | |
| **Health Care** | | | | | | | | |
| **Emergency** | | | | | | | | |
| **Dental** | | | | | | | | |
| **Vision** | | | | | | | | |
| **Miscellaneous Expense** | | | | | | | | |
| **Miscellaneous Expense** | | | | | | | | |
| **Miscellaneous Expense** | | | | | | | | |
| | | | | | | | | |
| **EXPENSES SUBTOTAL:** | | | | | | | | |
| | | | | | | | | |
| **CURRENTLY IN SAVING ACCOUNT:** | | | | | | | | |
| | | | | | | | | |
| **REMAIN IN CHECKING ACCOUNT:** | | | | | | | | |

# BASIC BUDGET WORK SHEET

| CATEGORY | Date Started: |
|---|---|
| **INCOME:** | |
| Wages (pay) | |
| Bonuses | |
| Interest income | |
| Capital gain income | |
| Miscellaneous income (for example: child support) | |
| INCOME SUBTOTAL: | |

*(YOUR SUBTOTAL WILL BECOME YOUR INCREASE AFTER YOU ADD UP YOUR INCOME.)*

| EXPENSES: | $ COST | DUE DATE | PAID | PARTIALLY PAID | NEED TO BE PAID ($ BALANCE) | TIME & DATE | REFERENCE/CONFIRMATION NUMBER | SUBTOTAL AFTER EACH PAYMENT |
|---|---|---|---|---|---|---|---|---|
| | | | | | | | | |
| Tithe | 10% | | | | | | | |
| Mortgage, Rent or Lease | | | | | | | | |
| Utilities: Gas/Water/Trash | | | | | | | | |
| Electricity | | | | | | | | |
| Telephone | | | | | | | | |
| Home: Repairs/Maintenance | | | | | | | | |
| Car(s)/Vehicle(s) Payment(s) | | | | | | | | |
| Entertainment | | | | | | | | |
| Auto Insurance | | | | | | | | |
| Transportation Maintenance/Repair | | | | | | | | |
| Vehicle(s) Gasoline | | | | | | | | |
| Child Care/Day Care | | | | | | | | |
| Groceries | | | | | | | | |

| | | | | | | | |
|---|---|---|---|---|---|---|---|
| **Other Transportation: Tolls, Bus, Subway, Etc.** | | | | | | | |
| **Toiletries/Household Products** | | | | | | | |
| **Allowance(s)** | | | | | | | |
| **College Tuition** | | | | | | | |
| **Clothing** | | | | | | | |
| **Eating Out** | | | | | | | |
| **Personal Property Tax** | | | | | | | |
| **Pets (Food and Care)** | | | | | | | |
| **Saving(s)** | | | | | | | |
| **Hobbies** | | | | | | | |
| **Gift(s)/Donation(s)** | | | | | | | |
| **Entertainment/Recreation** | | | | | | | |
| **Credit Card Payment(s)** | | | | | | | |
| **Health Care** | | | | | | | |
| **Emergency** | | | | | | | |
| **Dental** | | | | | | | |
| **Vision** | | | | | | | |
| **Miscellaneous Expense** | | | | | | | |
| **Miscellaneous Expense** | | | | | | | |
| **Miscellaneous Expense** | | | | | | | |
| | | | | | | | |
| **EXPENSES SUBTOTAL:** | | | | | | | |
| | | | | | | | |
| **CURRENTLY IN SAVING ACCOUNT:** | | | | | | | |
| | | | | | | | |
| **REMAIN IN CHECKING ACCOUNT:** | | | | | | | |

# BASIC BUDGET WORK SHEET

| CATEGORY | Date Started: |
|---|---|
| **INCOME:** | |

| | |
|---|---|
| **Wages (pay)** | |
| **Bonuses** | |
| **Interest income** | |
| **Capital gain income** | |
| **Miscellaneous income (for example: child support)** | |
| **INCOME SUBTOTAL:** | |

*(YOUR SUBTOTAL WILL BECOME YOUR INCREASE AFTER YOU ADD UP YOUR INCOME.)*

| EXPENSES: | $ COST | DUE DATE | PAID | PARTIALLY PAID | NEED TO BE PAID ($ BALANCE) | TIME & DATE | REFERENCE/CONFIRMATION NUMBER | SUBTOTAL AFTER EACH PAYMENT |
|---|---|---|---|---|---|---|---|---|
| | | | | | | | | |
| Tithe | 10% | | | | | | | |
| Mortgage, Rent or Lease | | | | | | | | |
| Utilities: Gas/Water/ Trash | | | | | | | | |
| Electricity | | | | | | | | |
| Telephone | | | | | | | | |
| Home: Repairs/Maintenance | | | | | | | | |
| Car(s)/Vehicle(s) Payment(s) | | | | | | | | |
| Entertainment | | | | | | | | |
| Auto Insurance | | | | | | | | |
| Transportation Maintenance/Repair | | | | | | | | |
| Vehicle(s) Gasoline | | | | | | | | |
| Child Care/Day Care | | | | | | | | |
| Groceries | | | | | | | | |

| | | | | | | | |
|---|---|---|---|---|---|---|---|
| Other Transportation: Tolls, Bus, Subway, Etc. | | | | | | | |
| Toiletries/Household Products | | | | | | | |
| Allowance(s) | | | | | | | |
| College Tuition | | | | | | | |
| Clothing | | | | | | | |
| Eating Out | | | | | | | |
| Personal Property Tax | | | | | | | |
| Pets (Food and Care) | | | | | | | |
| Saving(s) | | | | | | | |
| Hobbies | | | | | | | |
| Gift(s)/Donation(s) | | | | | | | |
| Entertainment/Recreation | | | | | | | |
| Credit Card Payment(s) | | | | | | | |
| Health Care | | | | | | | |
| Emergency | | | | | | | |
| Dental | | | | | | | |
| Vision | | | | | | | |
| Miscellaneous Expense | | | | | | | |
| Miscellaneous Expense | | | | | | | |
| Miscellaneous Expense | | | | | | | |
| | | | | | | | |
| EXPENSES SUBTOTAL: | | | | | | | |
| | | | | | | | |
| CURRENTLY IN SAVING ACCOUNT: | | | | | | | |
| | | | | | | | |
| REMAIN IN CHECKING ACCOUNT: | | | | | | | |

# BASIC BUDGET WORK SHEET

| CATEGORY | Date Started: |
|---|---|
| INCOME: | |
| Wages (pay) | |
| Bonuses | |
| Interest income | |
| Capital gain income | |
| Miscellaneous income (for example: child support) | |
| INCOME SUBTOTAL: | |

*(YOUR SUBTOTAL WILL BECOME YOUR INCREASE AFTER YOU ADD UP YOUR INCOME.)*

| EXPENSES: | $ COST | DUE DATE | PAID | PARTIALLY PAID | NEED TO BE PAID ($ BALANCE) | TIME & DATE | REFERENCE/CON FIRMATION NUMBER | SUBTOTAL AFTER EACH PAYMENT |
|---|---|---|---|---|---|---|---|---|
| | | | | | | | | |
| Tithe | 10% | | | | | | | |
| Mortgage, Rent or Lease | | | | | | | | |
| Utilities: Gas/Water/ Trash | | | | | | | | |
| Electricity | | | | | | | | |
| Telephone | | | | | | | | |
| Home: Repairs/Maintenance | | | | | | | | |
| Car(s)/Vehicle(s) Payment(s) | | | | | | | | |
| Entertainment | | | | | | | | |
| Auto Insurance | | | | | | | | |
| Transportation Maintenance/Repair | | | | | | | | |
| Vehicle(s) Gasoline | | | | | | | | |
| Child Care/Day Care | | | | | | | | |
| Groceries | | | | | | | | |

| | | | | | | | |
|---|---|---|---|---|---|---|---|
| **Other Transportation: Tolls, Bus, Subway, Etc.** | | | | | | | |
| **Toiletries/Household Products** | | | | | | | |
| **Allowance(s)** | | | | | | | |
| **College Tuition** | | | | | | | |
| **Clothing** | | | | | | | |
| **Eating Out** | | | | | | | |
| **Personal Property Tax** | | | | | | | |
| **Pets (Food and Care)** | | | | | | | |
| **Saving(s)** | | | | | | | |
| **Hobbies** | | | | | | | |
| **Gift(s)/Donation(s)** | | | | | | | |
| **Entertainment/Recreation** | | | | | | | |
| **Credit Card Payment(s)** | | | | | | | |
| **Health Care** | | | | | | | |
| **Emergency** | | | | | | | |
| **Dental** | | | | | | | |
| **Vision** | | | | | | | |
| **Miscellaneous Expense** | | | | | | | |
| **Miscellaneous Expense** | | | | | | | |
| **Miscellaneous Expense** | | | | | | | |
| | | | | | | | |
| **EXPENSES SUBTOTAL:** | | | | | | | |
| | | | | | | | |
| **CURRENTLY IN SAVING ACCOUNT:** | | | | | | | |
| | | | | | | | |
| **REMAIN IN CHECKING ACCOUNT:** | | | | | | | |

# Basic Budget Work Sheet

| Category | Date Started: |
|---|---|
| **INCOME:** | |
| | |
| Wages (pay) | |
| Bonuses | |
| Interest income | |
| Capital gain income | |
| Miscellaneous income (for example: child support) | |
| Income Subtotal: | |

*(Your subtotal will become your increase after you add up your income.)*

| Expenses: | $ Cost | Due Date | Paid | Partially Paid | Need to be Paid ($ Balance) | Time & Date | Reference/Confirmation Number | Subtotal After Each Payment |
|---|---|---|---|---|---|---|---|---|
| | | | | | | | | |
| Tithe | 10% | | | | | | | |
| Mortgage, Rent or Lease | | | | | | | | |
| Utilities: Gas/Water/ Trash | | | | | | | | |
| Electricity | | | | | | | | |
| Telephone | | | | | | | | |
| Home: Repairs/Maintenance | | | | | | | | |
| Car(s)/Vehicle(s) Payment(s) | | | | | | | | |
| Entertainment | | | | | | | | |
| Auto Insurance | | | | | | | | |
| Transportation Maintenance/Repair | | | | | | | | |
| Vehicle(s) Gasoline | | | | | | | | |
| Child Care/Day Care | | | | | | | | |
| Groceries | | | | | | | | |

| | | | | | | | |
|---|---|---|---|---|---|---|---|
| **Other Transportation: Tolls, Bus, Subway, Etc.** | | | | | | | |
| **Toiletries/Household Products** | | | | | | | |
| **Allowance(s)** | | | | | | | |
| **College Tuition** | | | | | | | |
| **Clothing** | | | | | | | |
| **Eating Out** | | | | | | | |
| **Personal Property Tax** | | | | | | | |
| **Pets (Food and Care)** | | | | | | | |
| **Saving(s)** | | | | | | | |
| **Hobbies** | | | | | | | |
| **Gift(s)/Donation(s)** | | | | | | | |
| **Entertainment/Recreation** | | | | | | | |
| **Credit Card Payment(s)** | | | | | | | |
| **Health Care** | | | | | | | |
| **Emergency** | | | | | | | |
| **Dental** | | | | | | | |
| **Vision** | | | | | | | |
| **Miscellaneous Expense** | | | | | | | |
| **Miscellaneous Expense** | | | | | | | |
| **Miscellaneous Expense** | | | | | | | |
| | | | | | | | |
| **EXPENSES SUBTOTAL:** | | | | | | | |
| | | | | | | | |
| **CURRENTLY IN SAVING ACCOUNT:** | | | | | | | |
| | | | | | | | |
| **REMAIN IN CHECKING ACCOUNT:** | | | | | | | |

# Basic Budget Work Sheet

| Category | Date Started: |
|---|---|
| | **Income:** |

| | |
|---|---|
| Wages (pay) | |
| Bonuses | |
| Interest income | |
| Capital gain income | |
| Miscellaneous income (for example: child support) | |
| Income Subtotal: | |

*(Your subtotal will become your increase after you add up your income.)*

| Expenses: | $ Cost | Due Date | Paid | Partially Paid | Need to be Paid ($ Balance) | Time & Date | Reference/Confirmation Number | Subtotal After Each Payment |
|---|---|---|---|---|---|---|---|---|
| | | | | | | | | |
| Tithe | 10% | | | | | | | |
| Mortgage, Rent or Lease | | | | | | | | |
| Utilities: Gas/Water/ Trash | | | | | | | | |
| Electricity | | | | | | | | |
| Telephone | | | | | | | | |
| Home: Repairs/Maintenance | | | | | | | | |
| Car(s)/Vehicle(s) Payment(s) | | | | | | | | |
| Entertainment | | | | | | | | |
| Auto Insurance | | | | | | | | |
| Transportation Maintenance/Repair | | | | | | | | |
| Vehicle(s) Gasoline | | | | | | | | |
| Child Care/Day Care | | | | | | | | |
| Groceries | | | | | | | | |

| | | | | | | | |
|---|---|---|---|---|---|---|---|
| **Other Transportation: Tolls, Bus, Subway, Etc.** | | | | | | | |
| **Toiletries/Household Products** | | | | | | | |
| **Allowance(s)** | | | | | | | |
| **College Tuition** | | | | | | | |
| **Clothing** | | | | | | | |
| **Eating Out** | | | | | | | |
| **Personal Property Tax** | | | | | | | |
| **Pets (Food and Care)** | | | | | | | |
| **Saving(s)** | | | | | | | |
| **Hobbies** | | | | | | | |
| **Gift(s)/Donation(s)** | | | | | | | |
| **Entertainment/Recreation** | | | | | | | |
| **Credit Card Payment(s)** | | | | | | | |
| **Health Care** | | | | | | | |
| **Emergency** | | | | | | | |
| **Dental** | | | | | | | |
| **Vision** | | | | | | | |
| **Miscellaneous Expense** | | | | | | | |
| **Miscellaneous Expense** | | | | | | | |
| **Miscellaneous Expense** | | | | | | | |
| | | | | | | | |
| **EXPENSES SUBTOTAL:** | | | | | | | |
| | | | | | | | |
| **CURRENTLY IN SAVING ACCOUNT:** | | | | | | | |
| | | | | | | | |
| **REMAIN IN CHECKING ACCOUNT:** | | | | | | | |

# BASIC BUDGET WORK SHEET

| CATEGORY | Date Started: |
|---|---|
| **INCOME:** | |
| Wages (pay) | |
| Bonuses | |
| Interest income | |
| Capital gain income | |
| Miscellaneous income (for example: child support) | |
| INCOME SUBTOTAL: | |

*(YOUR SUBTOTAL WILL BECOME YOUR INCREASE AFTER YOU ADD UP YOUR INCOME.)*

| EXPENSES: | $ COST | DUE DATE | PAID | PARTIALLY PAID | NEED TO BE PAID ($ BALANCE) | TIME & DATE | REFERENCE/CON FIRMATION NUMBER | SUBTOTAL AFTER EACH PAYMENT |
|---|---|---|---|---|---|---|---|---|
| | | | | | | | | |
| Tithe | 10% | | | | | | | |
| Mortgage, Rent or Lease | | | | | | | | |
| Utilities: Gas/Water/ Trash | | | | | | | | |
| Electricity | | | | | | | | |
| Telephone | | | | | | | | |
| Home: Repairs/Maintenance | | | | | | | | |
| Car(s)/Vehicle(s) Payment(s) | | | | | | | | |
| Entertainment | | | | | | | | |
| Auto Insurance | | | | | | | | |
| Transportation Maintenance/Repair | | | | | | | | |
| Vehicle(s) Gasoline | | | | | | | | |
| Child Care/Day Care | | | | | | | | |
| Groceries | | | | | | | | |

| | | | | | | | | |
|---|---|---|---|---|---|---|---|---|
| **Other Transportation: Tolls, Bus, Subway, Etc.** | | | | | | | | |
| **Toiletries/Household Products** | | | | | | | | |
| **Allowance(s)** | | | | | | | | |
| **College Tuition** | | | | | | | | |
| **Clothing** | | | | | | | | |
| **Eating Out** | | | | | | | | |
| **Personal Property Tax** | | | | | | | | |
| **Pets (Food and Care)** | | | | | | | | |
| **Saving(s)** | | | | | | | | |
| **Hobbies** | | | | | | | | |
| **Gift(s)/Donation(s)** | | | | | | | | |
| **Entertainment/Recreation** | | | | | | | | |
| **Credit Card Payment(s)** | | | | | | | | |
| **Health Care** | | | | | | | | |
| **Emergency** | | | | | | | | |
| **Dental** | | | | | | | | |
| **Vision** | | | | | | | | |
| **Miscellaneous Expense** | | | | | | | | |
| **Miscellaneous Expense** | | | | | | | | |
| **Miscellaneous Expense** | | | | | | | | |
| | | | | | | | | |
| **EXPENSES SUBTOTAL:** | | | | | | | | |
| | | | | | | | | |
| **CURRENTLY IN SAVING ACCOUNT:** | | | | | | | | |
| | | | | | | | | |
| **REMAIN IN CHECKING ACCOUNT:** | | | | | | | | |

# Basic Budget Work Sheet

| Category | Date Started: |
|---|---|
| | **INCOME:** |

| | |
|---|---|
| Wages (pay) | |
| Bonuses | |
| Interest income | |
| Capital gain income | |
| Miscellaneous income (for example: child support) | |
| INCOME SUBTOTAL: | |

*(Your subtotal will become your increase after you add up your income.)*

| Expenses: | $ Cost | Due Date | Paid | Partially Paid | Need to be Paid ($ Balance) | Time & Date | Reference/Confirmation Number | Subtotal After Each Payment |
|---|---|---|---|---|---|---|---|---|
| | | | | | | | | |
| Tithe | 10% | | | | | | | |
| Mortgage, Rent or Lease | | | | | | | | |
| Utilities: Gas/Water/Trash | | | | | | | | |
| Electricity | | | | | | | | |
| Telephone | | | | | | | | |
| Home: Repairs/Maintenance | | | | | | | | |
| Car(s)/Vehicle(s) Payment(s) | | | | | | | | |
| Entertainment | | | | | | | | |
| Auto Insurance | | | | | | | | |
| Transportation Maintenance/Repair | | | | | | | | |
| Vehicle(s) Gasoline | | | | | | | | |
| Child Care/Day Care | | | | | | | | |
| Groceries | | | | | | | | |

| | | | | | | | | |
|---|---|---|---|---|---|---|---|---|
| **Other Transportation: Tolls, Bus, Subway, Etc.** | | | | | | | | |
| **Toiletries/Household Products** | | | | | | | | |
| **Allowance(s)** | | | | | | | | |
| **College Tuition** | | | | | | | | |
| **Clothing** | | | | | | | | |
| **Eating Out** | | | | | | | | |
| **Personal Property Tax** | | | | | | | | |
| **Pets (Food and Care)** | | | | | | | | |
| **Saving(s)** | | | | | | | | |
| **Hobbies** | | | | | | | | |
| **Gift(s)/Donation(s)** | | | | | | | | |
| **Entertainment/Recreation** | | | | | | | | |
| **Credit Card Payment(s)** | | | | | | | | |
| **Health Care** | | | | | | | | |
| **Emergency** | | | | | | | | |
| **Dental** | | | | | | | | |
| **Vision** | | | | | | | | |
| **Miscellaneous Expense** | | | | | | | | |
| **Miscellaneous Expense** | | | | | | | | |
| **Miscellaneous Expense** | | | | | | | | |
| | | | | | | | | |
| **EXPENSES SUBTOTAL:** | | | | | | | | |
| | | | | | | | | |
| **CURRENTLY IN SAVING ACCOUNT:** | | | | | | | | |
| | | | | | | | | |
| **REMAIN IN CHECKING ACCOUNT:** | | | | | | | | |

# BASIC BUDGET WORK SHEET

| CATEGORY | Date Started: |
|---|---|
| **INCOME:** | |
| Wages (pay) | |
| Bonuses | |
| Interest income | |
| Capital gain income | |
| Miscellaneous income (for example: child support) | |
| INCOME SUBTOTAL: | |

*(YOUR SUBTOTAL WILL BECOME YOUR INCREASE AFTER YOU ADD UP YOUR INCOME.)*

| EXPENSES: | $ COST | DUE DATE | PAID | PARTIALLY PAID | NEED TO BE PAID ($ BALANCE) | TIME & DATE | REFERENCE/CONFIRMATION NUMBER | SUBTOTAL AFTER EACH PAYMENT |
|---|---|---|---|---|---|---|---|---|
| | | | | | | | | |
| Tithe | 10% | | | | | | | |
| Mortgage, Rent or Lease | | | | | | | | |
| Utilities: Gas/Water/Trash | | | | | | | | |
| Electricity | | | | | | | | |
| Telephone | | | | | | | | |
| Home: Repairs/Maintenance | | | | | | | | |
| Car(s)/Vehicle(s) Payment(s) | | | | | | | | |
| Entertainment | | | | | | | | |
| Auto Insurance | | | | | | | | |
| Transportation Maintenance/Repair | | | | | | | | |
| Vehicle(s) Gasoline | | | | | | | | |
| Child Care/Day Care | | | | | | | | |
| Groceries | | | | | | | | |

| | | | | | | | | |
|---|---|---|---|---|---|---|---|---|
| **Other Transportation: Tolls, Bus, Subway, Etc.** | | | | | | | | |
| **Toiletries/Household Products** | | | | | | | | |
| **Allowance(s)** | | | | | | | | |
| **College Tuition** | | | | | | | | |
| **Clothing** | | | | | | | | |
| **Eating Out** | | | | | | | | |
| **Personal Property Tax** | | | | | | | | |
| **Pets (Food and Care)** | | | | | | | | |
| **Saving(s)** | | | | | | | | |
| **Hobbies** | | | | | | | | |
| **Gift(s)/Donation(s)** | | | | | | | | |
| **Entertainment/Recreation** | | | | | | | | |
| **Credit Card Payment(s)** | | | | | | | | |
| **Health Care** | | | | | | | | |
| **Emergency** | | | | | | | | |
| **Dental** | | | | | | | | |
| **Vision** | | | | | | | | |
| **Miscellaneous Expense** | | | | | | | | |
| **Miscellaneous Expense** | | | | | | | | |
| **Miscellaneous Expense** | | | | | | | | |
| | | | | | | | | |
| **EXPENSES SUBTOTAL:** | | | | | | | | |
| | | | | | | | | |
| **CURRENTLY IN SAVING ACCOUNT:** | | | | | | | | |
| | | | | | | | | |
| **REMAIN IN CHECKING ACCOUNT:** | | | | | | | | |

# Basic Budget Work Sheet

| CATEGORY | Date Started: |
|---|---|

| INCOME: | |
|---|---|
| **Wages (pay)** | |
| **Bonuses** | |
| **Interest income** | |
| **Capital gain income** | |
| **Miscellaneous income (for example: child support)** | |
| **INCOME SUBTOTAL:** | |

*(YOUR SUBTOTAL WILL BECOME YOUR INCREASE AFTER YOU ADD UP YOUR INCOME.)*

| EXPENSES: | $ COST | DUE DATE | PAID | PARTIALLY PAID | NEED TO BE PAID ($ BALANCE) | TIME & DATE | REFERENCE/CONFIRMATION NUMBER | SUBTOTAL AFTER EACH PAYMENT |
|---|---|---|---|---|---|---|---|---|
| | | | | | | | | |
| **Tithe** | 10% | | | | | | | |
| **Mortgage, Rent or Lease** | | | | | | | | |
| **Utilities: Gas/Water/Trash** | | | | | | | | |
| **Electricity** | | | | | | | | |
| **Telephone** | | | | | | | | |
| **Home: Repairs/Maintenance** | | | | | | | | |
| **Car(s)/Vehicle(s) Payment(s)** | | | | | | | | |
| **Entertainment** | | | | | | | | |
| **Auto Insurance** | | | | | | | | |
| **Transportation Maintenance/Repair** | | | | | | | | |
| **Vehicle(s) Gasoline** | | | | | | | | |
| **Child Care/Day Care** | | | | | | | | |
| **Groceries** | | | | | | | | |

| | | | | | | | | |
|---|---|---|---|---|---|---|---|---|
| **Other Transportation: Tolls, Bus, Subway, Etc.** | | | | | | | | |
| **Toiletries/Household Products** | | | | | | | | |
| **Allowance(s)** | | | | | | | | |
| **College Tuition** | | | | | | | | |
| **Clothing** | | | | | | | | |
| **Eating Out** | | | | | | | | |
| **Personal Property Tax** | | | | | | | | |
| **Pets (Food and Care)** | | | | | | | | |
| **Saving(s)** | | | | | | | | |
| **Hobbies** | | | | | | | | |
| **Gift(s)/Donation(s)** | | | | | | | | |
| **Entertainment/Recreation** | | | | | | | | |
| **Credit Card Payment(s)** | | | | | | | | |
| **Health Care** | | | | | | | | |
| **Emergency** | | | | | | | | |
| **Dental** | | | | | | | | |
| **Vision** | | | | | | | | |
| **Miscellaneous Expense** | | | | | | | | |
| **Miscellaneous Expense** | | | | | | | | |
| **Miscellaneous Expense** | | | | | | | | |
| | | | | | | | | |
| **EXPENSES SUBTOTAL:** | | | | | | | | |
| | | | | | | | | |
| **CURRENTLY IN SAVING ACCOUNT:** | | | | | | | | |
| | | | | | | | | |
| **REMAIN IN CHECKING ACCOUNT:** | | | | | | | | |

# BASIC BUDGET WORK SHEET

| CATEGORY | Date Started: _____ |
|---|---|
| | **INCOME:** |

| | |
|---|---|
| **Wages (pay)** | |
| **Bonuses** | |
| **Interest income** | |
| **Capital gain income** | |
| **Miscellaneous income (for example: child support)** | |
| **INCOME SUBTOTAL:** | |

*(YOUR SUBTOTAL WILL BECOME YOUR INCREASE AFTER YOU ADD UP YOUR INCOME.)*

| EXPENSES: | $ COST | DUE DATE | PAID | PARTIALLY PAID | NEED TO BE PAID ($ BALANCE) | TIME & DATE | REFERENCE/CON FIRMATION NUMBER | SUBTOTAL AFTER EACH PAYMENT |
|---|---|---|---|---|---|---|---|---|
| | | | | | | | | |
| **Tithe** | 10% | | | | | | | |
| **Mortgage, Rent or Lease** | | | | | | | | |
| **Utilities: Gas/Water/ Trash** | | | | | | | | |
| **Electricity** | | | | | | | | |
| **Telephone** | | | | | | | | |
| **Home: Repairs/Maintenance** | | | | | | | | |
| **Car(s)/Vehicle(s) Payment(s)** | | | | | | | | |
| **Entertainment** | | | | | | | | |
| **Auto Insurance** | | | | | | | | |
| **Transportation Maintenance/Repair** | | | | | | | | |
| **Vehicle(s) Gasoline** | | | | | | | | |
| **Child Care/Day Care** | | | | | | | | |
| **Groceries** | | | | | | | | |

| | | | | | | | |
|---|---|---|---|---|---|---|---|
| **Other Transportation: Tolls, Bus, Subway, Etc.** | | | | | | | |
| **Toiletries/Household Products** | | | | | | | |
| **Allowance(s)** | | | | | | | |
| **College Tuition** | | | | | | | |
| **Clothing** | | | | | | | |
| **Eating Out** | | | | | | | |
| **Personal Property Tax** | | | | | | | |
| **Pets (Food and Care)** | | | | | | | |
| **Saving(s)** | | | | | | | |
| **Hobbies** | | | | | | | |
| **Gift(s)/Donation(s)** | | | | | | | |
| **Entertainment/Recreation** | | | | | | | |
| **Credit Card Payment(s)** | | | | | | | |
| **Health Care** | | | | | | | |
| **Emergency** | | | | | | | |
| **Dental** | | | | | | | |
| **Vision** | | | | | | | |
| **Miscellaneous Expense** | | | | | | | |
| **Miscellaneous Expense** | | | | | | | |
| **Miscellaneous Expense** | | | | | | | |
| | | | | | | | |
| **EXPENSES SUBTOTAL:** | | | | | | | |
| | | | | | | | |
| **CURRENTLY IN SAVING ACCOUNT:** | | | | | | | |
| | | | | | | | |
| **REMAIN IN CHECKING ACCOUNT:** | | | | | | | |

# BASIC BUDGET WORK SHEET

| CATEGORY | Date Started: _____ |
|---|---|
| INCOME: | |
| | |
| Wages (pay) | |
| Bonuses | |
| Interest income | |
| Capital gain income | |
| Miscellaneous income (for example: child support) | |
| INCOME SUBTOTAL: | |
| *(YOUR SUBTOTAL WILL BECOME YOUR INCREASE AFTER YOU ADD UP YOUR INCOME.)* | |

| EXPENSES: | $ COST | DUE DATE | PAID | PARTIALLY PAID | NEED TO BE PAID ($ BALANCE) | TIME & DATE | REFERENCE/CON FIRMATION NUMBER | SUBTOTAL AFTER EACH PAYMENT |
|---|---|---|---|---|---|---|---|---|
| | | | | | | | | |
| Tithe | 10% | | | | | | | |
| Mortgage, Rent or Lease | | | | | | | | |
| Utilities: Gas/Water/ Trash | | | | | | | | |
| Electricity | | | | | | | | |
| Telephone | | | | | | | | |
| Home: Repairs/Maintenance | | | | | | | | |
| Car(s)/Vehicle(s) Payment(s) | | | | | | | | |
| Entertainment | | | | | | | | |
| Auto Insurance | | | | | | | | |
| Transportation Maintenance/Repair | | | | | | | | |
| Vehicle(s) Gasoline | | | | | | | | |
| Child Care/Day Care | | | | | | | | |
| Groceries | | | | | | | | |

| | | | | | | | |
|---|---|---|---|---|---|---|---|
| Other Transportation: Tolls, Bus, Subway, Etc. | | | | | | | |
| Toiletries/Household Products | | | | | | | |
| Allowance(s) | | | | | | | |
| College Tuition | | | | | | | |
| Clothing | | | | | | | |
| Eating Out | | | | | | | |
| Personal Property Tax | | | | | | | |
| Pets (Food and Care) | | | | | | | |
| Saving(s) | | | | | | | |
| Hobbies | | | | | | | |
| Gift(s)/Donation(s) | | | | | | | |
| Entertainment/Recreation | | | | | | | |
| Credit Card Payment(s) | | | | | | | |
| Health Care | | | | | | | |
| Emergency | | | | | | | |
| Dental | | | | | | | |
| Vision | | | | | | | |
| Miscellaneous Expense | | | | | | | |
| Miscellaneous Expense | | | | | | | |
| Miscellaneous Expense | | | | | | | |
| | | | | | | | |
| EXPENSES SUBTOTAL: | | | | | | | |
| | | | | | | | |
| CURRENTLY IN SAVING ACCOUNT: | | | | | | | |
| | | | | | | | |
| REMAIN IN CHECKING ACCOUNT: | | | | | | | |

# BASIC BUDGET WORK SHEET

| CATEGORY | Date Started: |
|---|---|
| **INCOME:** | |
| | |
| Wages (pay) | |
| Bonuses | |
| Interest income | |
| Capital gain income | |
| Miscellaneous income (for example: child support) | |
| INCOME SUBTOTAL: | |
| *(YOUR SUBTOTAL WILL BECOME YOUR INCREASE AFTER YOU ADD UP YOUR INCOME.)* | |

| EXPENSES: | $ COST | DUE DATE | PAID | PARTIALLY PAID | NEED TO BE PAID ($ BALANCE) | TIME & DATE | REFERENCE/CONFIRMATION NUMBER | SUBTOTAL AFTER EACH PAYMENT |
|---|---|---|---|---|---|---|---|---|
| | | | | | | | | |
| Tithe | 10% | | | | | | | |
| Mortgage, Rent or Lease | | | | | | | | |
| Utilities: Gas/Water/Trash | | | | | | | | |
| Electricity | | | | | | | | |
| Telephone | | | | | | | | |
| Home: Repairs/Maintenance | | | | | | | | |
| Car(s)/Vehicle(s) Payment(s) | | | | | | | | |
| Entertainment | | | | | | | | |
| Auto Insurance | | | | | | | | |
| Transportation Maintenance/Repair | | | | | | | | |
| Vehicle(s) Gasoline | | | | | | | | |
| Child Care/Day Care | | | | | | | | |
| Groceries | | | | | | | | |

| | | | | | | | |
|---|---|---|---|---|---|---|---|
| **Other Transportation: Tolls, Bus, Subway, Etc.** | | | | | | | |
| **Toiletries/Household Products** | | | | | | | |
| **Allowance(s)** | | | | | | | |
| **College Tuition** | | | | | | | |
| **Clothing** | | | | | | | |
| **Eating Out** | | | | | | | |
| **Personal Property Tax** | | | | | | | |
| **Pets (Food and Care)** | | | | | | | |
| **Saving(s)** | | | | | | | |
| **Hobbies** | | | | | | | |
| **Gift(s)/Donation(s)** | | | | | | | |
| **Entertainment/Recreation** | | | | | | | |
| **Credit Card Payment(s)** | | | | | | | |
| **Health Care** | | | | | | | |
| **Emergency** | | | | | | | |
| **Dental** | | | | | | | |
| **Vision** | | | | | | | |
| **Miscellaneous Expense** | | | | | | | |
| **Miscellaneous Expense** | | | | | | | |
| **Miscellaneous Expense** | | | | | | | |
| | | | | | | | |
| **EXPENSES SUBTOTAL:** | | | | | | | |
| | | | | | | | |
| **CURRENTLY IN SAVING ACCOUNT:** | | | | | | | |
| | | | | | | | |
| **REMAIN IN CHECKING ACCOUNT:** | | | | | | | |

# BASIC BUDGET WORK SHEET

| CATEGORY | Date Started: |
|---|---|
| **INCOME:** | |
| Wages (pay) | |
| Bonuses | |
| Interest income | |
| Capital gain income | |
| Miscellaneous income (for example: child support) | |
| INCOME SUBTOTAL: | |
| *(YOUR SUBTOTAL WILL BECOME YOUR INCREASE AFTER YOU ADD UP YOUR INCOME.)* | |

| EXPENSES: | $ COST | DUE DATE | PAID | PARTIALLY PAID | NEED TO BE PAID ($ BALANCE) | TIME & DATE | REFERENCE/CON FIRMATION NUMBER | SUBTOTAL AFTER EACH PAYMENT |
|---|---|---|---|---|---|---|---|---|
| | | | | | | | | |
| Tithe | 10% | | | | | | | |
| Mortgage, Rent or Lease | | | | | | | | |
| Utilities: Gas/Water/ Trash | | | | | | | | |
| Electricity | | | | | | | | |
| Telephone | | | | | | | | |
| Home: Repairs/Maintenance | | | | | | | | |
| Car(s)/Vehicle(s) Payment(s) | | | | | | | | |
| Entertainment | | | | | | | | |
| Auto Insurance | | | | | | | | |
| Transportation Maintenance/Repair | | | | | | | | |
| Vehicle(s) Gasoline | | | | | | | | |
| Child Care/Day Care | | | | | | | | |
| Groceries | | | | | | | | |

| | | | | | | | |
|---|---|---|---|---|---|---|---|
| **Other Transportation: Tolls, Bus, Subway, Etc.** | | | | | | | |
| **Toiletries/Household Products** | | | | | | | |
| **Allowance(s)** | | | | | | | |
| **College Tuition** | | | | | | | |
| **Clothing** | | | | | | | |
| **Eating Out** | | | | | | | |
| **Personal Property Tax** | | | | | | | |
| **Pets (Food and Care)** | | | | | | | |
| **Saving(s)** | | | | | | | |
| **Hobbies** | | | | | | | |
| **Gift(s)/Donation(s)** | | | | | | | |
| **Entertainment/Recreation** | | | | | | | |
| **Credit Card Payment(s)** | | | | | | | |
| **Health Care** | | | | | | | |
| **Emergency** | | | | | | | |
| **Dental** | | | | | | | |
| **Vision** | | | | | | | |
| **Miscellaneous Expense** | | | | | | | |
| **Miscellaneous Expense** | | | | | | | |
| **Miscellaneous Expense** | | | | | | | |
| | | | | | | | |
| **EXPENSES SUBTOTAL:** | | | | | | | |
| | | | | | | | |
| **CURRENTLY IN SAVING ACCOUNT:** | | | | | | | |
| | | | | | | | |
| **REMAIN IN CHECKING ACCOUNT:** | | | | | | | |

# BASIC BUDGET WORK SHEET

| CATEGORY | Date Started: |
|---|---|
| **INCOME:** | |
| | |
| Wages (pay) | |
| Bonuses | |
| Interest income | |
| Capital gain income | |
| Miscellaneous income (for example: child support) | |
| INCOME SUBTOTAL: | |
| *(YOUR SUBTOTAL WILL BECOME YOUR INCREASE AFTER YOU ADD UP YOUR INCOME.)* | |
| | |

| EXPENSES: | $ COST | DUE DATE | PAID | PARTIALLY PAID | NEED TO BE PAID ($ BALANCE) | TIME & DATE | REFERENCE/CONFIRMATION NUMBER | SUBTOTAL AFTER EACH PAYMENT |
|---|---|---|---|---|---|---|---|---|
| | | | | | | | | |
| Tithe | 10% | | | | | | | |
| Mortgage, Rent or Lease | | | | | | | | |
| Utilities: Gas/Water/Trash | | | | | | | | |
| Electricity | | | | | | | | |
| Telephone | | | | | | | | |
| Home: Repairs/Maintenance | | | | | | | | |
| Car(s)/Vehicle(s) Payment(s) | | | | | | | | |
| Entertainment | | | | | | | | |
| Auto Insurance | | | | | | | | |
| Transportation Maintenance/Repair | | | | | | | | |
| Vehicle(s) Gasoline | | | | | | | | |
| Child Care/Day Care | | | | | | | | |
| Groceries | | | | | | | | |

| | | | | | | | |
|---|---|---|---|---|---|---|---|
| **Other Transportation: Tolls, Bus, Subway, Etc.** | | | | | | | |
| **Toiletries/Household Products** | | | | | | | |
| **Allowance(s)** | | | | | | | |
| **College Tuition** | | | | | | | |
| **Clothing** | | | | | | | |
| **Eating Out** | | | | | | | |
| **Personal Property Tax** | | | | | | | |
| **Pets (Food and Care)** | | | | | | | |
| **Saving(s)** | | | | | | | |
| **Hobbies** | | | | | | | |
| **Gift(s)/Donation(s)** | | | | | | | |
| **Entertainment/Recreation** | | | | | | | |
| **Credit Card Payment(s)** | | | | | | | |
| **Health Care** | | | | | | | |
| **Emergency** | | | | | | | |
| **Dental** | | | | | | | |
| **Vision** | | | | | | | |
| **Miscellaneous Expense** | | | | | | | |
| **Miscellaneous Expense** | | | | | | | |
| **Miscellaneous Expense** | | | | | | | |
| | | | | | | | |
| **EXPENSES SUBTOTAL:** | | | | | | | |
| | | | | | | | |
| **CURRENTLY IN SAVING ACCOUNT:** | | | | | | | |
| | | | | | | | |
| **REMAIN IN CHECKING ACCOUNT:** | | | | | | | |

# Basic Budget Work Sheet

| CATEGORY | Date Started: |
|---|---|
| **INCOME:** | |
| Wages (pay) | |
| Bonuses | |
| Interest income | |
| Capital gain income | |
| Miscellaneous income (for example: child support) | |
| INCOME SUBTOTAL: | |
| *(YOUR SUBTOTAL WILL BECOME YOUR INCREASE AFTER YOU ADD UP YOUR INCOME.)* | |

| EXPENSES: | $ COST | DUE DATE | PAID | PARTIALLY PAID | NEED TO BE PAID ($ BALANCE) | TIME & DATE | REFERENCE/CON FIRMATION NUMBER | SUBTOTAL AFTER EACH PAYMENT |
|---|---|---|---|---|---|---|---|---|
| | | | | | | | | |
| Tithe | 10% | | | | | | | |
| Mortgage, Rent or Lease | | | | | | | | |
| Utilities: Gas/Water/ Trash | | | | | | | | |
| Electricity | | | | | | | | |
| Telephone | | | | | | | | |
| Home: Repairs/Maintenance | | | | | | | | |
| Car(s)/Vehicle(s) Payment(s) | | | | | | | | |
| Entertainment | | | | | | | | |
| Auto Insurance | | | | | | | | |
| Transportation Maintenance/Repair | | | | | | | | |
| Vehicle(s) Gasoline | | | | | | | | |
| Child Care/Day Care | | | | | | | | |
| Groceries | | | | | | | | |

| | | | | | | | |
|---|---|---|---|---|---|---|---|
| **Other Transportation: Tolls, Bus, Subway, Etc.** | | | | | | | |
| **Toiletries/Household Products** | | | | | | | |
| **Allowance(s)** | | | | | | | |
| **College Tuition** | | | | | | | |
| **Clothing** | | | | | | | |
| **Eating Out** | | | | | | | |
| **Personal Property Tax** | | | | | | | |
| **Pets (Food and Care)** | | | | | | | |
| **Saving(s)** | | | | | | | |
| **Hobbies** | | | | | | | |
| **Gift(s)/Donation(s)** | | | | | | | |
| **Entertainment/Recreation** | | | | | | | |
| **Credit Card Payment(s)** | | | | | | | |
| **Health Care** | | | | | | | |
| **Emergency** | | | | | | | |
| **Dental** | | | | | | | |
| **Vision** | | | | | | | |
| **Miscellaneous Expense** | | | | | | | |
| **Miscellaneous Expense** | | | | | | | |
| **Miscellaneous Expense** | | | | | | | |
| | | | | | | | |
| **EXPENSES SUBTOTAL:** | | | | | | | |
| | | | | | | | |
| **CURRENTLY IN SAVING ACCOUNT:** | | | | | | | |
| | | | | | | | |
| **REMAIN IN CHECKING ACCOUNT:** | | | | | | | |

# BASIC BUDGET WORK SHEET

| CATEGORY | Date Started: |
|---|---|

| INCOME: | |
|---|---|
| Wages (pay) | |
| Bonuses | |
| Interest income | |
| Capital gain income | |
| Miscellaneous income (for example: child support) | |
| INCOME SUBTOTAL: | |

*(YOUR SUBTOTAL WILL BECOME YOUR INCREASE AFTER YOU ADD UP YOUR INCOME.)*

| EXPENSES: | $ COST | DUE DATE | PAID | PARTIALLY PAID | NEED TO BE PAID ($ BALANCE) | TIME & DATE | REFERENCE/CON FIRMATION NUMBER | SUBTOTAL AFTER EACH PAYMENT |
|---|---|---|---|---|---|---|---|---|
| | | | | | | | | |
| Tithe | 10% | | | | | | | |
| Mortgage, Rent or Lease | | | | | | | | |
| Utilities: Gas/Water/ Trash | | | | | | | | |
| Electricity | | | | | | | | |
| Telephone | | | | | | | | |
| Home: Repairs/Maintenance | | | | | | | | |
| Car(s)/Vehicle(s) Payment(s) | | | | | | | | |
| Entertainment | | | | | | | | |
| Auto Insurance | | | | | | | | |
| Transportation Maintenance/Repair | | | | | | | | |
| Vehicle(s) Gasoline | | | | | | | | |
| Child Care/Day Care | | | | | | | | |
| Groceries | | | | | | | | |

| | | | | | | | | |
|---|---|---|---|---|---|---|---|---|
| **Other Transportation: Tolls, Bus, Subway, Etc.** | | | | | | | | |
| **Toiletries/Household Products** | | | | | | | | |
| **Allowance(s)** | | | | | | | | |
| **College Tuition** | | | | | | | | |
| **Clothing** | | | | | | | | |
| **Eating Out** | | | | | | | | |
| **Personal Property Tax** | | | | | | | | |
| **Pets (Food and Care)** | | | | | | | | |
| **Saving(s)** | | | | | | | | |
| **Hobbies** | | | | | | | | |
| **Gift(s)/Donation(s)** | | | | | | | | |
| **Entertainment/Recreation** | | | | | | | | |
| **Credit Card Payment(s)** | | | | | | | | |
| **Health Care** | | | | | | | | |
| **Emergency** | | | | | | | | |
| **Dental** | | | | | | | | |
| **Vision** | | | | | | | | |
| **Miscellaneous Expense** | | | | | | | | |
| **Miscellaneous Expense** | | | | | | | | |
| **Miscellaneous Expense** | | | | | | | | |
| | | | | | | | | |
| **EXPENSES SUBTOTAL:** | | | | | | | | |
| | | | | | | | | |
| **CURRENTLY IN SAVING ACCOUNT:** | | | | | | | | |
| | | | | | | | | |
| **REMAIN IN CHECKING ACCOUNT:** | | | | | | | | |

## Basic Budget Work Sheet

| CATEGORY | Date Started: |
|---|---|
| **INCOME:** | |
| Wages (pay) | |
| Bonuses | |
| Interest income | |
| Capital gain income | |
| Miscellaneous income (for example: child support) | |
| INCOME SUBTOTAL: | |
| *(YOUR SUBTOTAL WILL BECOME YOUR INCREASE AFTER YOU ADD UP YOUR INCOME.)* | |

| EXPENSES: | $ COST | DUE DATE | PAID | PARTIALLY PAID | NEED TO BE PAID ($ BALANCE) | TIME & DATE | REFERENCE/CON FIRMATION NUMBER | SUBTOTAL AFTER EACH PAYMENT |
|---|---|---|---|---|---|---|---|---|
| | | | | | | | | |
| Tithe | 10% | | | | | | | |
| Mortgage, Rent or Lease | | | | | | | | |
| Utilities: Gas/Water/Trash | | | | | | | | |
| Electricity | | | | | | | | |
| Telephone | | | | | | | | |
| Home: Repairs/Maintenance | | | | | | | | |
| Car(s)/Vehicle(s) Payment(s) | | | | | | | | |
| Entertainment | | | | | | | | |
| Auto Insurance | | | | | | | | |
| Transportation Maintenance/Repair | | | | | | | | |
| Vehicle(s) Gasoline | | | | | | | | |
| Child Care/Day Care | | | | | | | | |
| Groceries | | | | | | | | |

| | | | | | | | |
|---|---|---|---|---|---|---|---|
| **Other Transportation: Tolls, Bus, Subway, Etc.** | | | | | | | |
| **Toiletries/Household Products** | | | | | | | |
| **Allowance(s)** | | | | | | | |
| **College Tuition** | | | | | | | |
| **Clothing** | | | | | | | |
| **Eating Out** | | | | | | | |
| **Personal Property Tax** | | | | | | | |
| **Pets (Food and Care)** | | | | | | | |
| **Saving(s)** | | | | | | | |
| **Hobbies** | | | | | | | |
| **Gift(s)/Donation(s)** | | | | | | | |
| **Entertainment/Recreation** | | | | | | | |
| **Credit Card Payment(s)** | | | | | | | |
| **Health Care** | | | | | | | |
| **Emergency** | | | | | | | |
| **Dental** | | | | | | | |
| **Vision** | | | | | | | |
| **Miscellaneous Expense** | | | | | | | |
| **Miscellaneous Expense** | | | | | | | |
| **Miscellaneous Expense** | | | | | | | |
| | | | | | | | |
| **EXPENSES SUBTOTAL:** | | | | | | | |
| | | | | | | | |
| **CURRENTLY IN SAVING ACCOUNT:** | | | | | | | |
| | | | | | | | |
| **REMAIN IN CHECKING ACCOUNT:** | | | | | | | |

## Basic Budget Work Sheet

| CATEGORY | Date Started: _____ |
|---|---|
| **INCOME:** | |
| | |
| Wages (pay) | |
| Bonuses | |
| Interest income | |
| Capital gain income | |
| Miscellaneous income (for example: child support) | |
| INCOME SUBTOTAL: | |

*(YOUR SUBTOTAL WILL BECOME YOUR INCREASE AFTER YOU ADD UP YOUR INCOME.)*

| EXPENSES: | $ COST | DUE DATE | PAID | PARTIALLY PAID | NEED TO BE PAID ($ BALANCE) | TIME & DATE | REFERENCE/CON FIRMATION NUMBER | SUBTOTAL AFTER EACH PAYMENT |
|---|---|---|---|---|---|---|---|---|
| | | | | | | | | |
| Tithe | 10% | | | | | | | |
| Mortgage, Rent or Lease | | | | | | | | |
| Utilities: Gas/Water/ Trash | | | | | | | | |
| Electricity | | | | | | | | |
| Telephone | | | | | | | | |
| Home: Repairs/Maintenance | | | | | | | | |
| Car(s)/Vehicle(s) Payment(s) | | | | | | | | |
| Entertainment | | | | | | | | |
| Auto Insurance | | | | | | | | |
| Transportation Maintenance/Repair | | | | | | | | |
| Vehicle(s) Gasoline | | | | | | | | |
| Child Care/Day Care | | | | | | | | |
| Groceries | | | | | | | | |

| | | | | | | | |
|---|---|---|---|---|---|---|---|
| **Other Transportation: Tolls, Bus, Subway, Etc.** | | | | | | | |
| **Toiletries/Household Products** | | | | | | | |
| **Allowance(s)** | | | | | | | |
| **College Tuition** | | | | | | | |
| **Clothing** | | | | | | | |
| **Eating Out** | | | | | | | |
| **Personal Property Tax** | | | | | | | |
| **Pets (Food and Care)** | | | | | | | |
| **Saving(s)** | | | | | | | |
| **Hobbies** | | | | | | | |
| **Gift(s)/Donation(s)** | | | | | | | |
| **Entertainment/Recreation** | | | | | | | |
| **Credit Card Payment(s)** | | | | | | | |
| **Health Care** | | | | | | | |
| **Emergency** | | | | | | | |
| **Dental** | | | | | | | |
| **Vision** | | | | | | | |
| **Miscellaneous Expense** | | | | | | | |
| **Miscellaneous Expense** | | | | | | | |
| **Miscellaneous Expense** | | | | | | | |
| | | | | | | | |
| **EXPENSES SUBTOTAL:** | | | | | | | |
| | | | | | | | |
| **CURRENTLY IN SAVING ACCOUNT:** | | | | | | | |
| | | | | | | | |
| **REMAIN IN CHECKING ACCOUNT:** | | | | | | | |

# BASIC BUDGET WORK SHEET

| CATEGORY | Date Started: _____ |
|---|---|
| INCOME: | |
| Wages (pay) | |
| Bonuses | |
| Interest income | |
| Capital gain income | |
| Miscellaneous income (for example: child support) | |
| INCOME SUBTOTAL: | |
| *(YOUR SUBTOTAL WILL BECOME YOUR INCREASE AFTER YOU ADD UP YOUR INCOME.)* | |

| EXPENSES: | $ COST | DUE DATE | PAID | PARTIALLY PAID | NEED TO BE PAID ($ BALANCE) | TIME & DATE | REFERENCE/CON FIRMATION NUMBER | SUBTOTAL AFTER EACH PAYMENT |
|---|---|---|---|---|---|---|---|---|
| | | | | | | | | |
| Tithe | 10% | | | | | | | |
| Mortgage, Rent or Lease | | | | | | | | |
| Utilities: Gas/Water/ Trash | | | | | | | | |
| Electricity | | | | | | | | |
| Telephone | | | | | | | | |
| Home: Repairs/Maintenance | | | | | | | | |
| Car(s)/Vehicle(s) Payment(s) | | | | | | | | |
| Entertainment | | | | | | | | |
| Auto Insurance | | | | | | | | |
| Transportation Maintenance/Repair | | | | | | | | |
| Vehicle(s) Gasoline | | | | | | | | |
| Child Care/Day Care | | | | | | | | |
| Groceries | | | | | | | | |

| | | | | | | | |
|---|---|---|---|---|---|---|---|
| **Other Transportation: Tolls, Bus, Subway, Etc.** | | | | | | | |
| **Toiletries/Household Products** | | | | | | | |
| **Allowance(s)** | | | | | | | |
| **College Tuition** | | | | | | | |
| **Clothing** | | | | | | | |
| **Eating Out** | | | | | | | |
| **Personal Property Tax** | | | | | | | |
| **Pets (Food and Care)** | | | | | | | |
| **Saving(s)** | | | | | | | |
| **Hobbies** | | | | | | | |
| **Gift(s)/Donation(s)** | | | | | | | |
| **Entertainment/Recreation** | | | | | | | |
| **Credit Card Payment(s)** | | | | | | | |
| **Health Care** | | | | | | | |
| **Emergency** | | | | | | | |
| **Dental** | | | | | | | |
| **Vision** | | | | | | | |
| **Miscellaneous Expense** | | | | | | | |
| **Miscellaneous Expense** | | | | | | | |
| **Miscellaneous Expense** | | | | | | | |
| | | | | | | | |
| **EXPENSES SUBTOTAL:** | | | | | | | |
| | | | | | | | |
| **CURRENTLY IN SAVING ACCOUNT:** | | | | | | | |
| | | | | | | | |
| **REMAIN IN CHECKING ACCOUNT:** | | | | | | | |

# BASIC BUDGET WORK SHEET

| CATEGORY | Date Started: |
|---|---|
| **INCOME:** | |
| Wages (pay) | |
| Bonuses | |
| Interest income | |
| Capital gain income | |
| Miscellaneous income (for example: child support) | |
| INCOME SUBTOTAL: | |

*(YOUR SUBTOTAL WILL BECOME YOUR INCREASE AFTER YOU ADD UP YOUR INCOME.)*

| EXPENSES: | $ COST | DUE DATE | PAID | PARTIALLY PAID | NEED TO BE PAID ($ BALANCE) | TIME & DATE | REFERENCE/CONFIRMATION NUMBER | SUBTOTAL AFTER EACH PAYMENT |
|---|---|---|---|---|---|---|---|---|
| | | | | | | | | |
| Tithe | 10% | | | | | | | |
| Mortgage, Rent or Lease | | | | | | | | |
| Utilities: Gas/Water/ Trash | | | | | | | | |
| Electricity | | | | | | | | |
| Telephone | | | | | | | | |
| Home: Repairs/Maintenance | | | | | | | | |
| Car(s)/Vehicle(s) Payment(s) | | | | | | | | |
| Entertainment | | | | | | | | |
| Auto Insurance | | | | | | | | |
| Transportation Maintenance/Repair | | | | | | | | |
| Vehicle(s) Gasoline | | | | | | | | |
| Child Care/Day Care | | | | | | | | |
| Groceries | | | | | | | | |

| | | | | | | | |
|---|---|---|---|---|---|---|---|
| **Other Transportation: Tolls, Bus, Subway, Etc.** | | | | | | | |
| **Toiletries/Household Products** | | | | | | | |
| **Allowance(s)** | | | | | | | |
| **College Tuition** | | | | | | | |
| **Clothing** | | | | | | | |
| **Eating Out** | | | | | | | |
| **Personal Property Tax** | | | | | | | |
| **Pets (Food and Care)** | | | | | | | |
| **Saving(s)** | | | | | | | |
| **Hobbies** | | | | | | | |
| **Gift(s)/Donation(s)** | | | | | | | |
| **Entertainment/Recreation** | | | | | | | |
| **Credit Card Payment(s)** | | | | | | | |
| **Health Care** | | | | | | | |
| **Emergency** | | | | | | | |
| **Dental** | | | | | | | |
| **Vision** | | | | | | | |
| **Miscellaneous Expense** | | | | | | | |
| **Miscellaneous Expense** | | | | | | | |
| **Miscellaneous Expense** | | | | | | | |
| | | | | | | | |
| **EXPENSES SUBTOTAL:** | | | | | | | |
| | | | | | | | |
| **CURRENTLY IN SAVING ACCOUNT:** | | | | | | | |
| | | | | | | | |
| **REMAIN IN CHECKING ACCOUNT:** | | | | | | | |

# BASIC BUDGET WORK SHEET

| CATEGORY | Date Started: |
|---|---|
| INCOME: | |
| | |
| Wages (pay) | |
| Bonuses | |
| Interest income | |
| Capital gain income | |
| Miscellaneous income (for example: child support) | |
| INCOME SUBTOTAL: | |

*(YOUR SUBTOTAL WILL BECOME YOUR INCREASE AFTER YOU ADD UP YOUR INCOME.)*

| EXPENSES: | $ COST | DUE DATE | PAID | PARTIALLY PAID | NEED TO BE PAID ($ BALANCE) | TIME & DATE | REFERENCE/CONFIRMATION NUMBER | SUBTOTAL AFTER EACH PAYMENT |
|---|---|---|---|---|---|---|---|---|
| | | | | | | | | |
| Tithe | 10% | | | | | | | |
| Mortgage, Rent or Lease | | | | | | | | |
| Utilities: Gas/Water/ Trash | | | | | | | | |
| Electricity | | | | | | | | |
| Telephone | | | | | | | | |
| Home: Repairs/Maintenance | | | | | | | | |
| Car(s)/Vehicle(s) Payment(s) | | | | | | | | |
| Entertainment | | | | | | | | |
| Auto Insurance | | | | | | | | |
| Transportation Maintenance/Repair | | | | | | | | |
| Vehicle(s) Gasoline | | | | | | | | |
| Child Care/Day Care | | | | | | | | |
| Groceries | | | | | | | | |

| | | | | | | | | |
|---|---|---|---|---|---|---|---|---|
| **Other Transportation: Tolls, Bus, Subway, Etc.** | | | | | | | | |
| **Toiletries/Household Products** | | | | | | | | |
| **Allowance(s)** | | | | | | | | |
| **College Tuition** | | | | | | | | |
| **Clothing** | | | | | | | | |
| **Eating Out** | | | | | | | | |
| **Personal Property Tax** | | | | | | | | |
| **Pets (Food and Care)** | | | | | | | | |
| **Saving(s)** | | | | | | | | |
| **Hobbies** | | | | | | | | |
| **Gift(s)/Donation(s)** | | | | | | | | |
| **Entertainment/Recreation** | | | | | | | | |
| **Credit Card Payment(s)** | | | | | | | | |
| **Health Care** | | | | | | | | |
| **Emergency** | | | | | | | | |
| **Dental** | | | | | | | | |
| **Vision** | | | | | | | | |
| **Miscellaneous Expense** | | | | | | | | |
| **Miscellaneous Expense** | | | | | | | | |
| **Miscellaneous Expense** | | | | | | | | |
| | | | | | | | | |
| **EXPENSES SUBTOTAL:** | | | | | | | | |
| | | | | | | | | |
| **CURRENTLY IN SAVING ACCOUNT:** | | | | | | | | |
| | | | | | | | | |
| **REMAIN IN CHECKING ACCOUNT:** | | | | | | | | |

# Basic Budget Work Sheet

| CATEGORY | Date Started: |
|---|---|
| INCOME: | |
| | |
| Wages (pay) | |
| Bonuses | |
| Interest income | |
| Capital gain income | |
| Miscellaneous income (for example: child support) | |
| INCOME SUBTOTAL: | |
| *(YOUR SUBTOTAL WILL BECOME YOUR INCREASE AFTER YOU ADD UP YOUR INCOME.)* | |

| EXPENSES: | $ COST | DUE DATE | PAID | PARTIALLY PAID | NEED TO BE PAID ($ BALANCE) | TIME & DATE | REFERENCE/CON FIRMATION NUMBER | SUBTOTAL AFTER EACH PAYMENT |
|---|---|---|---|---|---|---|---|---|
| | | | | | | | | |
| Tithe | 10% | | | | | | | |
| Mortgage, Rent or Lease | | | | | | | | |
| Utilities: Gas/Water/Trash | | | | | | | | |
| Electricity | | | | | | | | |
| Telephone | | | | | | | | |
| Home: Repairs/Maintenance | | | | | | | | |
| Car(s)/Vehicle(s) Payment(s) | | | | | | | | |
| Entertainment | | | | | | | | |
| Auto Insurance | | | | | | | | |
| Transportation Maintenance/Repair | | | | | | | | |
| Vehicle(s) Gasoline | | | | | | | | |
| Child Care/Day Care | | | | | | | | |
| Groceries | | | | | | | | |

| | | | | | | | | |
|---|---|---|---|---|---|---|---|---|
| **Other Transportation: Tolls, Bus, Subway, Etc.** | | | | | | | | |
| **Toiletries/Household Products** | | | | | | | | |
| **Allowance(s)** | | | | | | | | |
| **College Tuition** | | | | | | | | |
| **Clothing** | | | | | | | | |
| **Eating Out** | | | | | | | | |
| **Personal Property Tax** | | | | | | | | |
| **Pets (Food and Care)** | | | | | | | | |
| **Saving(s)** | | | | | | | | |
| **Hobbies** | | | | | | | | |
| **Gift(s)/Donation(s)** | | | | | | | | |
| **Entertainment/Recreation** | | | | | | | | |
| **Credit Card Payment(s)** | | | | | | | | |
| **Health Care** | | | | | | | | |
| **Emergency** | | | | | | | | |
| **Dental** | | | | | | | | |
| **Vision** | | | | | | | | |
| **Miscellaneous Expense** | | | | | | | | |
| **Miscellaneous Expense** | | | | | | | | |
| **Miscellaneous Expense** | | | | | | | | |
| | | | | | | | | |
| **EXPENSES SUBTOTAL:** | | | | | | | | |
| | | | | | | | | |
| **CURRENTLY IN SAVING ACCOUNT:** | | | | | | | | |
| | | | | | | | | |
| **REMAIN IN CHECKING ACCOUNT:** | | | | | | | | |

# Basic Budget Work Sheet

| CATEGORY | Date Started: |
|---|---|
| **INCOME:** | |
| | |
| Wages (pay) | |
| Bonuses | |
| Interest income | |
| Capital gain income | |
| Miscellaneous income (for example: child support) | |
| INCOME SUBTOTAL: | |
| *(YOUR SUBTOTAL WILL BECOME YOUR INCREASE AFTER YOU ADD UP YOUR INCOME.)* | |

| EXPENSES: | $ COST | DUE DATE | PAID | PARTIALLY PAID | NEED TO BE PAID ($ BALANCE) | TIME & DATE | REFERENCE/CON FIRMATION NUMBER | SUBTOTAL AFTER EACH PAYMENT |
|---|---|---|---|---|---|---|---|---|
| | | | | | | | | |
| Tithe | 10% | | | | | | | |
| Mortgage, Rent or Lease | | | | | | | | |
| Utilities: Gas/Water/ Trash | | | | | | | | |
| Electricity | | | | | | | | |
| Telephone | | | | | | | | |
| Home: Repairs/Maintenance | | | | | | | | |
| Car(s)/Vehicle(s) Payment(s) | | | | | | | | |
| Entertainment | | | | | | | | |
| Auto Insurance | | | | | | | | |
| Transportation Maintenance/Repair | | | | | | | | |
| Vehicle(s) Gasoline | | | | | | | | |
| Child Care/Day Care | | | | | | | | |
| Groceries | | | | | | | | |

| | | | | | | | | |
|---|---|---|---|---|---|---|---|---|
| Other Transportation: Tolls, Bus, Subway, Etc. | | | | | | | | |
| Toiletries/Household Products | | | | | | | | |
| Allowance(s) | | | | | | | | |
| College Tuition | | | | | | | | |
| Clothing | | | | | | | | |
| Eating Out | | | | | | | | |
| Personal Property Tax | | | | | | | | |
| Pets (Food and Care) | | | | | | | | |
| Saving(s) | | | | | | | | |
| Hobbies | | | | | | | | |
| Gift(s)/Donation(s) | | | | | | | | |
| Entertainment/Recreation | | | | | | | | |
| Credit Card Payment(s) | | | | | | | | |
| Health Care | | | | | | | | |
| Emergency | | | | | | | | |
| Dental | | | | | | | | |
| Vision | | | | | | | | |
| Miscellaneous Expense | | | | | | | | |
| Miscellaneous Expense | | | | | | | | |
| Miscellaneous Expense | | | | | | | | |
| | | | | | | | | |
| EXPENSES SUBTOTAL: | | | | | | | | |
| | | | | | | | | |
| CURRENTLY IN SAVING ACCOUNT: | | | | | | | | |
| | | | | | | | | |
| REMAIN IN CHECKING ACCOUNT: | | | | | | | | |

# BASIC BUDGET WORK SHEET

| CATEGORY | Date Started: |
|---|---|
| **INCOME:** | |
| Wages (pay) | |
| Bonuses | |
| Interest income | |
| Capital gain income | |
| Miscellaneous income (for example: child support) | |
| INCOME SUBTOTAL: | |

*(YOUR SUBTOTAL WILL BECOME YOUR INCREASE AFTER YOU ADD UP YOUR INCOME.)*

| EXPENSES: | $ COST | DUE DATE | PAID | PARTIALLY PAID | NEED TO BE PAID ($ BALANCE) | TIME & DATE | REFERENCE/CON FIRMATION NUMBER | SUBTOTAL AFTER EACH PAYMENT |
|---|---|---|---|---|---|---|---|---|
| | | | | | | | | |
| Tithe | 10% | | | | | | | |
| Mortgage, Rent or Lease | | | | | | | | |
| Utilities: Gas/Water/ Trash | | | | | | | | |
| Electricity | | | | | | | | |
| Telephone | | | | | | | | |
| Home: Repairs/Maintenance | | | | | | | | |
| Car(s)/Vehicle(s) Payment(s) | | | | | | | | |
| Entertainment | | | | | | | | |
| Auto Insurance | | | | | | | | |
| Transportation Maintenance/Repair | | | | | | | | |
| Vehicle(s) Gasoline | | | | | | | | |
| Child Care/Day Care | | | | | | | | |
| Groceries | | | | | | | | |

| | | | | | | | |
|---|---|---|---|---|---|---|---|
| **Other Transportation: Tolls, Bus, Subway, Etc.** | | | | | | | |
| **Toiletries/Household Products** | | | | | | | |
| **Allowance(s)** | | | | | | | |
| **College Tuition** | | | | | | | |
| **Clothing** | | | | | | | |
| **Eating Out** | | | | | | | |
| **Personal Property Tax** | | | | | | | |
| **Pets (Food and Care)** | | | | | | | |
| **Saving(s)** | | | | | | | |
| **Hobbies** | | | | | | | |
| **Gift(s)/Donation(s)** | | | | | | | |
| **Entertainment/Recreation** | | | | | | | |
| **Credit Card Payment(s)** | | | | | | | |
| **Health Care** | | | | | | | |
| **Emergency** | | | | | | | |
| **Dental** | | | | | | | |
| **Vision** | | | | | | | |
| **Miscellaneous Expense** | | | | | | | |
| **Miscellaneous Expense** | | | | | | | |
| **Miscellaneous Expense** | | | | | | | |
| | | | | | | | |
| **EXPENSES SUBTOTAL:** | | | | | | | |
| | | | | | | | |
| **CURRENTLY IN SAVING ACCOUNT:** | | | | | | | |
| | | | | | | | |
| **REMAIN IN CHECKING ACCOUNT:** | | | | | | | |

# BASIC BUDGET WORK SHEET

| CATEGORY | Date Started: |
|---|---|
| **INCOME:** | |
| Wages (pay) | |
| Bonuses | |
| Interest income | |
| Capital gain income | |
| Miscellaneous income (for example: child support) | |
| **INCOME SUBTOTAL:** | |

*(YOUR SUBTOTAL WILL BECOME YOUR INCREASE AFTER YOU ADD UP YOUR INCOME.)*

| EXPENSES: | $ COST | DUE DATE | PAID | PARTIALLY PAID | NEED TO BE PAID ($ BALANCE) | TIME & DATE | REFERENCE/CON FIRMATION NUMBER | SUBTOTAL AFTER EACH PAYMENT |
|---|---|---|---|---|---|---|---|---|
| | | | | | | | | |
| Tithe | 10% | | | | | | | |
| Mortgage, Rent or Lease | | | | | | | | |
| Utilities: Gas/Water/ Trash | | | | | | | | |
| Electricity | | | | | | | | |
| Telephone | | | | | | | | |
| Home: Repairs/Maintenance | | | | | | | | |
| Car(s)/Vehicle(s) Payment(s) | | | | | | | | |
| Entertainment | | | | | | | | |
| Auto Insurance | | | | | | | | |
| Transportation Maintenance/Repair | | | | | | | | |
| Vehicle(s) Gasoline | | | | | | | | |
| Child Care/Day Care | | | | | | | | |
| Groceries | | | | | | | | |

| | | | | | | | |
|---|---|---|---|---|---|---|---|
| **Other Transportation: Tolls, Bus, Subway, Etc.** | | | | | | | |
| **Toiletries/Household Products** | | | | | | | |
| **Allowance(s)** | | | | | | | |
| **College Tuition** | | | | | | | |
| **Clothing** | | | | | | | |
| **Eating Out** | | | | | | | |
| **Personal Property Tax** | | | | | | | |
| **Pets (Food and Care)** | | | | | | | |
| **Saving(s)** | | | | | | | |
| **Hobbies** | | | | | | | |
| **Gift(s)/Donation(s)** | | | | | | | |
| **Entertainment/Recreation** | | | | | | | |
| **Credit Card Payment(s)** | | | | | | | |
| **Health Care** | | | | | | | |
| **Emergency** | | | | | | | |
| **Dental** | | | | | | | |
| **Vision** | | | | | | | |
| **Miscellaneous Expense** | | | | | | | |
| **Miscellaneous Expense** | | | | | | | |
| **Miscellaneous Expense** | | | | | | | |
| | | | | | | | |
| **EXPENSES SUBTOTAL:** | | | | | | | |
| | | | | | | | |
| **CURRENTLY IN SAVING ACCOUNT:** | | | | | | | |
| | | | | | | | |
| **REMAIN IN CHECKING ACCOUNT:** | | | | | | | |

# Basic Budget Work Sheet

| CATEGORY | Date Started: |
|---|---|
| **INCOME:** | |

| | |
|---|---|
| Wages (pay) | |
| Bonuses | |
| Interest income | |
| Capital gain income | |
| Miscellaneous income (for example: child support) | |
| INCOME SUBTOTAL: | |

*(YOUR SUBTOTAL WILL BECOME YOUR INCREASE AFTER YOU ADD UP YOUR INCOME.)*

| EXPENSES: | $ COST | DUE DATE | PAID | PARTIALLY PAID | NEED TO BE PAID ($ BALANCE) | TIME & DATE | REFERENCE/CONFIRMATION NUMBER | SUBTOTAL AFTER EACH PAYMENT |
|---|---|---|---|---|---|---|---|---|
| | | | | | | | | |
| Tithe | 10% | | | | | | | |
| Mortgage, Rent or Lease | | | | | | | | |
| Utilities: Gas/Water/ Trash | | | | | | | | |
| Electricity | | | | | | | | |
| Telephone | | | | | | | | |
| Home: Repairs/Maintenance | | | | | | | | |
| Car(s)/Vehicle(s) Payment(s) | | | | | | | | |
| Entertainment | | | | | | | | |
| Auto Insurance | | | | | | | | |
| Transportation Maintenance/Repair | | | | | | | | |
| Vehicle(s) Gasoline | | | | | | | | |
| Child Care/Day Care | | | | | | | | |
| Groceries | | | | | | | | |

| | | | | | | | | |
|---|---|---|---|---|---|---|---|---|
| Other Transportation: Tolls, Bus, Subway, Etc. | | | | | | | | |
| Toiletries/Household Products | | | | | | | | |
| Allowance(s) | | | | | | | | |
| College Tuition | | | | | | | | |
| Clothing | | | | | | | | |
| Eating Out | | | | | | | | |
| Personal Property Tax | | | | | | | | |
| Pets (Food and Care) | | | | | | | | |
| Saving(s) | | | | | | | | |
| Hobbies | | | | | | | | |
| Gift(s)/Donation(s) | | | | | | | | |
| Entertainment/Recreation | | | | | | | | |
| Credit Card Payment(s) | | | | | | | | |
| Health Care | | | | | | | | |
| Emergency | | | | | | | | |
| Dental | | | | | | | | |
| Vision | | | | | | | | |
| Miscellaneous Expense | | | | | | | | |
| Miscellaneous Expense | | | | | | | | |
| Miscellaneous Expense | | | | | | | | |
| | | | | | | | | |
| EXPENSES SUBTOTAL: | | | | | | | | |
| | | | | | | | | |
| CURRENTLY IN SAVING ACCOUNT: | | | | | | | | |
| | | | | | | | | |
| REMAIN IN CHECKING ACCOUNT: | | | | | | | | |

# BASIC BUDGET WORK SHEET

| CATEGORY | Date Started: _____ |
|---|---|
| INCOME: | |
| Wages (pay) | |
| Bonuses | |
| Interest income | |
| Capital gain income | |
| Miscellaneous income (for example: child support) | |
| INCOME SUBTOTAL: | |
| *(YOUR SUBTOTAL WILL BECOME YOUR INCREASE AFTER YOU ADD UP YOUR INCOME.)* | |

| EXPENSES: | $ COST | DUE DATE | PAID | PARTIALLY PAID | NEED TO BE PAID ($ BALANCE) | TIME & DATE | REFERENCE/CONFIRMATION NUMBER | SUBTOTAL AFTER EACH PAYMENT |
|---|---|---|---|---|---|---|---|---|
| | | | | | | | | |
| Tithe | 10% | | | | | | | |
| Mortgage, Rent or Lease | | | | | | | | |
| Utilities: Gas/Water/ Trash | | | | | | | | |
| Electricity | | | | | | | | |
| Telephone | | | | | | | | |
| Home: Repairs/Maintenance | | | | | | | | |
| Car(s)/Vehicle(s) Payment(s) | | | | | | | | |
| Entertainment | | | | | | | | |
| Auto Insurance | | | | | | | | |
| Transportation Maintenance/Repair | | | | | | | | |
| Vehicle(s) Gasoline | | | | | | | | |
| Child Care/Day Care | | | | | | | | |
| Groceries | | | | | | | | |

| | | | | | | | |
|---|---|---|---|---|---|---|---|
| **Other Transportation: Tolls, Bus, Subway, Etc.** | | | | | | | |
| **Toiletries/Household Products** | | | | | | | |
| **Allowance(s)** | | | | | | | |
| **College Tuition** | | | | | | | |
| **Clothing** | | | | | | | |
| **Eating Out** | | | | | | | |
| **Personal Property Tax** | | | | | | | |
| **Pets (Food and Care)** | | | | | | | |
| **Saving(s)** | | | | | | | |
| **Hobbies** | | | | | | | |
| **Gift(s)/Donation(s)** | | | | | | | |
| **Entertainment/Recreation** | | | | | | | |
| **Credit Card Payment(s)** | | | | | | | |
| **Health Care** | | | | | | | |
| **Emergency** | | | | | | | |
| **Dental** | | | | | | | |
| **Vision** | | | | | | | |
| **Miscellaneous Expense** | | | | | | | |
| **Miscellaneous Expense** | | | | | | | |
| **Miscellaneous Expense** | | | | | | | |
| | | | | | | | |
| **EXPENSES SUBTOTAL:** | | | | | | | |
| | | | | | | | |
| **CURRENTLY IN SAVING ACCOUNT:** | | | | | | | |
| | | | | | | | |
| **REMAIN IN CHECKING ACCOUNT:** | | | | | | | |

# Basic Budget Work Sheet

| CATEGORY | Date Started: |
|---|---|
| **INCOME:** | |
| Wages (pay) | |
| Bonuses | |
| Interest income | |
| Capital gain income | |
| Miscellaneous income (for example: child support) | |
| INCOME SUBTOTAL: | |

*(YOUR SUBTOTAL WILL BECOME YOUR INCREASE AFTER YOU ADD UP YOUR INCOME.)*

| EXPENSES: | $ COST | DUE DATE | PAID | PARTIALLY PAID | NEED TO BE PAID ($ BALANCE) | TIME & DATE | REFERENCE/CONFIRMATION NUMBER | SUBTOTAL AFTER EACH PAYMENT |
|---|---|---|---|---|---|---|---|---|
| | | | | | | | | |
| Tithe | 10% | | | | | | | |
| Mortgage, Rent or Lease | | | | | | | | |
| Utilities: Gas/Water/Trash | | | | | | | | |
| Electricity | | | | | | | | |
| Telephone | | | | | | | | |
| Home: Repairs/Maintenance | | | | | | | | |
| Car(s)/Vehicle(s) Payment(s) | | | | | | | | |
| Entertainment | | | | | | | | |
| Auto Insurance | | | | | | | | |
| Transportation Maintenance/Repair | | | | | | | | |
| Vehicle(s) Gasoline | | | | | | | | |
| Child Care/Day Care | | | | | | | | |
| Groceries | | | | | | | | |

| | | | | | | | | |
|---|---|---|---|---|---|---|---|---|
| **Other Transportation: Tolls, Bus, Subway, Etc.** | | | | | | | | |
| **Toiletries/Household Products** | | | | | | | | |
| **Allowance(s)** | | | | | | | | |
| **College Tuition** | | | | | | | | |
| **Clothing** | | | | | | | | |
| **Eating Out** | | | | | | | | |
| **Personal Property Tax** | | | | | | | | |
| **Pets (Food and Care)** | | | | | | | | |
| **Saving(s)** | | | | | | | | |
| **Hobbies** | | | | | | | | |
| **Gift(s)/Donation(s)** | | | | | | | | |
| **Entertainment/Recreation** | | | | | | | | |
| **Credit Card Payment(s)** | | | | | | | | |
| **Health Care** | | | | | | | | |
| **Emergency** | | | | | | | | |
| **Dental** | | | | | | | | |
| **Vision** | | | | | | | | |
| **Miscellaneous Expense** | | | | | | | | |
| **Miscellaneous Expense** | | | | | | | | |
| **Miscellaneous Expense** | | | | | | | | |
| | | | | | | | | |
| **EXPENSES SUBTOTAL:** | | | | | | | | |
| | | | | | | | | |
| **CURRENTLY IN SAVING ACCOUNT:** | | | | | | | | |
| | | | | | | | | |
| **REMAIN IN CHECKING ACCOUNT:** | | | | | | | | |

# BASIC BUDGET WORK SHEET

| CATEGORY | Date Started: |
|---|---|
| **INCOME:** | |

| | |
|---|---|
| Wages (pay) | |
| Bonuses | |
| Interest income | |
| Capital gain income | |
| Miscellaneous income (for example: child support) | |
| INCOME SUBTOTAL: | |

*(YOUR SUBTOTAL WILL BECOME YOUR INCREASE AFTER YOU ADD UP YOUR INCOME.)*

| EXPENSES: | $ COST | DUE DATE | PAID | PARTIALLY PAID | NEED TO BE PAID ($ BALANCE) | TIME & DATE | REFERENCE/CONFIRMATION NUMBER | SUBTOTAL AFTER EACH PAYMENT |
|---|---|---|---|---|---|---|---|---|
| | | | | | | | | |
| Tithe | 10% | | | | | | | |
| Mortgage, Rent or Lease | | | | | | | | |
| Utilities: Gas/Water/Trash | | | | | | | | |
| Electricity | | | | | | | | |
| Telephone | | | | | | | | |
| Home: Repairs/Maintenance | | | | | | | | |
| Car(s)/Vehicle(s) Payment(s) | | | | | | | | |
| Entertainment | | | | | | | | |
| Auto Insurance | | | | | | | | |
| Transportation Maintenance/Repair | | | | | | | | |
| Vehicle(s) Gasoline | | | | | | | | |
| Child Care/Day Care | | | | | | | | |
| Groceries | | | | | | | | |

| | | | | | | | |
|---|---|---|---|---|---|---|---|
| **Other Transportation: Tolls, Bus, Subway, Etc.** | | | | | | | |
| **Toiletries/Household Products** | | | | | | | |
| **Allowance(s)** | | | | | | | |
| **College Tuition** | | | | | | | |
| **Clothing** | | | | | | | |
| **Eating Out** | | | | | | | |
| **Personal Property Tax** | | | | | | | |
| **Pets (Food and Care)** | | | | | | | |
| **Saving(s)** | | | | | | | |
| **Hobbies** | | | | | | | |
| **Gift(s)/Donation(s)** | | | | | | | |
| **Entertainment/Recreation** | | | | | | | |
| **Credit Card Payment(s)** | | | | | | | |
| **Health Care** | | | | | | | |
| **Emergency** | | | | | | | |
| **Dental** | | | | | | | |
| **Vision** | | | | | | | |
| **Miscellaneous Expense** | | | | | | | |
| **Miscellaneous Expense** | | | | | | | |
| **Miscellaneous Expense** | | | | | | | |
| | | | | | | | |
| **EXPENSES SUBTOTAL:** | | | | | | | |
| | | | | | | | |
| **CURRENTLY IN SAVING ACCOUNT:** | | | | | | | |
| | | | | | | | |
| **REMAIN IN CHECKING ACCOUNT:** | | | | | | | |

# Basic Budget Work Sheet

| CATEGORY | Date Started: _____ |
|---|---|
| **INCOME:** | |
| | |
| Wages (pay) | |
| Bonuses | |
| Interest income | |
| Capital gain income | |
| Miscellaneous income (for example: child support) | |
| INCOME SUBTOTAL: | |

*(YOUR SUBTOTAL WILL BECOME YOUR INCREASE AFTER YOU ADD UP YOUR INCOME.)*

| EXPENSES: | $ COST | DUE DATE | PAID | PARTIALLY PAID | NEED TO BE PAID ($ BALANCE) | TIME & DATE | REFERENCE/CON FIRMATION NUMBER | SUBTOTAL AFTER EACH PAYMENT |
|---|---|---|---|---|---|---|---|---|
| | | | | | | | | |
| Tithe | 10% | | | | | | | |
| Mortgage, Rent or Lease | | | | | | | | |
| Utilities: Gas/Water/ Trash | | | | | | | | |
| Electricity | | | | | | | | |
| Telephone | | | | | | | | |
| Home: Repairs/Maintenance | | | | | | | | |
| Car(s)/Vehicle(s) Payment(s) | | | | | | | | |
| Entertainment | | | | | | | | |
| Auto Insurance | | | | | | | | |
| Transportation Maintenance/Repair | | | | | | | | |
| Vehicle(s) Gasoline | | | | | | | | |
| Child Care/Day Care | | | | | | | | |
| Groceries | | | | | | | | |

| | | | | | | | | |
|---|---|---|---|---|---|---|---|---|
| Other Transportation: Tolls, Bus, Subway, Etc. | | | | | | | | |
| Toiletries/Household Products | | | | | | | | |
| Allowance(s) | | | | | | | | |
| College Tuition | | | | | | | | |
| Clothing | | | | | | | | |
| Eating Out | | | | | | | | |
| Personal Property Tax | | | | | | | | |
| Pets (Food and Care) | | | | | | | | |
| Saving(s) | | | | | | | | |
| Hobbies | | | | | | | | |
| Gift(s)/Donation(s) | | | | | | | | |
| Entertainment/Recreation | | | | | | | | |
| Credit Card Payment(s) | | | | | | | | |
| Health Care | | | | | | | | |
| Emergency | | | | | | | | |
| Dental | | | | | | | | |
| Vision | | | | | | | | |
| Miscellaneous Expense | | | | | | | | |
| Miscellaneous Expense | | | | | | | | |
| Miscellaneous Expense | | | | | | | | |
| | | | | | | | | |
| EXPENSES SUBTOTAL: | | | | | | | | |
| | | | | | | | | |
| CURRENTLY IN SAVING ACCOUNT: | | | | | | | | |
| | | | | | | | | |
| REMAIN IN CHECKING ACCOUNT: | | | | | | | | |

# BASIC BUDGET WORK SHEET

| CATEGORY | Date Started: |
|---|---|
| **INCOME:** | |
| | |
| Wages (pay) | |
| Bonuses | |
| Interest income | |
| Capital gain income | |
| Miscellaneous income (for example: child support) | |
| INCOME SUBTOTAL: | |

*(YOUR SUBTOTAL WILL BECOME YOUR INCREASE AFTER YOU ADD UP YOUR INCOME.)*

| EXPENSES: | $ COST | DUE DATE | PAID | PARTIALLY PAID | NEED TO BE PAID ($ BALANCE) | TIME & DATE | REFERENCE/CONFIRMATION NUMBER | SUBTOTAL AFTER EACH PAYMENT |
|---|---|---|---|---|---|---|---|---|
| | | | | | | | | |
| Tithe | 10% | | | | | | | |
| Mortgage, Rent or Lease | | | | | | | | |
| Utilities: Gas/Water/Trash | | | | | | | | |
| Electricity | | | | | | | | |
| Telephone | | | | | | | | |
| Home: Repairs/Maintenance | | | | | | | | |
| Car(s)/Vehicle(s) Payment(s) | | | | | | | | |
| Entertainment | | | | | | | | |
| Auto Insurance | | | | | | | | |
| Transportation Maintenance/Repair | | | | | | | | |
| Vehicle(s) Gasoline | | | | | | | | |
| Child Care/Day Care | | | | | | | | |
| Groceries | | | | | | | | |

| | | | | | | | | |
|---|---|---|---|---|---|---|---|---|
| **Other Transportation: Tolls, Bus, Subway, Etc.** | | | | | | | | |
| **Toiletries/Household Products** | | | | | | | | |
| **Allowance(s)** | | | | | | | | |
| **College Tuition** | | | | | | | | |
| **Clothing** | | | | | | | | |
| **Eating Out** | | | | | | | | |
| **Personal Property Tax** | | | | | | | | |
| **Pets (Food and Care)** | | | | | | | | |
| **Saving(s)** | | | | | | | | |
| **Hobbies** | | | | | | | | |
| **Gift(s)/Donation(s)** | | | | | | | | |
| **Entertainment/Recreation** | | | | | | | | |
| **Credit Card Payment(s)** | | | | | | | | |
| **Health Care** | | | | | | | | |
| **Emergency** | | | | | | | | |
| **Dental** | | | | | | | | |
| **Vision** | | | | | | | | |
| **Miscellaneous Expense** | | | | | | | | |
| **Miscellaneous Expense** | | | | | | | | |
| **Miscellaneous Expense** | | | | | | | | |
| | | | | | | | | |
| **EXPENSES SUBTOTAL:** | | | | | | | | |
| | | | | | | | | |
| **CURRENTLY IN SAVING ACCOUNT:** | | | | | | | | |
| | | | | | | | | |
| **REMAIN IN CHECKING ACCOUNT:** | | | | | | | | |

# BASIC BUDGET WORK SHEET

| CATEGORY | Date Started: _____ |
|----------|-------------------------------|
| **INCOME:** | |
| Wages (pay) | |
| Bonuses | |
| Interest income | |
| Capital gain income | |
| Miscellaneous income (for example: child support) | |
| INCOME SUBTOTAL: | |
| *(YOUR SUBTOTAL WILL BECOME YOUR INCREASE AFTER YOU ADD UP YOUR INCOME.)* | |

| EXPENSES: | $ COST | DUE DATE | PAID | PARTIALLY PAID | NEED TO BE PAID ($ BALANCE) | TIME & DATE | REFERENCE/CONFIRMATION NUMBER | SUBTOTAL AFTER EACH PAYMENT |
|-----------|--------|----------|------|----------------|------------------------------|-------------|-------------------------------|------------------------------|
| | | | | | | | | |
| Tithe | 10% | | | | | | | |
| Mortgage, Rent or Lease | | | | | | | | |
| Utilities: Gas/Water/Trash | | | | | | | | |
| Electricity | | | | | | | | |
| Telephone | | | | | | | | |
| Home: Repairs/Maintenance | | | | | | | | |
| Car(s)/Vehicle(s) Payment(s) | | | | | | | | |
| Entertainment | | | | | | | | |
| Auto Insurance | | | | | | | | |
| Transportation Maintenance/Repair | | | | | | | | |
| Vehicle(s) Gasoline | | | | | | | | |
| Child Care/Day Care | | | | | | | | |
| Groceries | | | | | | | | |

| | | | | | | | | |
|---|---|---|---|---|---|---|---|---|
| **Other Transportation: Tolls, Bus, Subway, Etc.** | | | | | | | | |
| **Toiletries/Household Products** | | | | | | | | |
| **Allowance(s)** | | | | | | | | |
| **College Tuition** | | | | | | | | |
| **Clothing** | | | | | | | | |
| **Eating Out** | | | | | | | | |
| **Personal Property Tax** | | | | | | | | |
| **Pets (Food and Care)** | | | | | | | | |
| **Saving(s)** | | | | | | | | |
| **Hobbies** | | | | | | | | |
| **Gift(s)/Donation(s)** | | | | | | | | |
| **Entertainment/Recreation** | | | | | | | | |
| **Credit Card Payment(s)** | | | | | | | | |
| **Health Care** | | | | | | | | |
| **Emergency** | | | | | | | | |
| **Dental** | | | | | | | | |
| **Vision** | | | | | | | | |
| **Miscellaneous Expense** | | | | | | | | |
| **Miscellaneous Expense** | | | | | | | | |
| **Miscellaneous Expense** | | | | | | | | |
| | | | | | | | | |
| **EXPENSES SUBTOTAL:** | | | | | | | | |
| | | | | | | | | |
| **CURRENTLY IN SAVING ACCOUNT:** | | | | | | | | |
| | | | | | | | | |
| **REMAIN IN CHECKING ACCOUNT:** | | | | | | | | |

# Basic Budget Work Sheet

| Category | Date Started: |
|---|---|
| **Income:** | |
| Wages (pay) | |
| Bonuses | |
| Interest income | |
| Capital gain income | |
| Miscellaneous income (for example: child support) | |
| **Income Subtotal:** | |

*(Your subtotal will become your increase after you add up your income.)*

| Expenses: | $ Cost | Due Date | Paid | Partially Paid | Need to be Paid ($ Balance) | Time & Date | Reference/Confirmation Number | Subtotal After Each Payment |
|---|---|---|---|---|---|---|---|---|
| | | | | | | | | |
| Tithe | 10% | | | | | | | |
| Mortgage, Rent or Lease | | | | | | | | |
| Utilities: Gas/Water/Trash | | | | | | | | |
| Electricity | | | | | | | | |
| Telephone | | | | | | | | |
| Home: Repairs/Maintenance | | | | | | | | |
| Car(s)/Vehicle(s) Payment(s) | | | | | | | | |
| Entertainment | | | | | | | | |
| Auto Insurance | | | | | | | | |
| Transportation Maintenance/Repair | | | | | | | | |
| Vehicle(s) Gasoline | | | | | | | | |
| Child Care/Day Care | | | | | | | | |
| Groceries | | | | | | | | |

| | | | | | | | | |
|---|---|---|---|---|---|---|---|---|
| **Other Transportation: Tolls, Bus, Subway, Etc.** | | | | | | | | |
| **Toiletries/Household Products** | | | | | | | | |
| **Allowance(s)** | | | | | | | | |
| **College Tuition** | | | | | | | | |
| **Clothing** | | | | | | | | |
| **Eating Out** | | | | | | | | |
| **Personal Property Tax** | | | | | | | | |
| **Pets (Food and Care)** | | | | | | | | |
| **Saving(s)** | | | | | | | | |
| **Hobbies** | | | | | | | | |
| **Gift(s)/Donation(s)** | | | | | | | | |
| **Entertainment/Recreation** | | | | | | | | |
| **Credit Card Payment(s)** | | | | | | | | |
| **Health Care** | | | | | | | | |
| **Emergency** | | | | | | | | |
| **Dental** | | | | | | | | |
| **Vision** | | | | | | | | |
| **Miscellaneous Expense** | | | | | | | | |
| **Miscellaneous Expense** | | | | | | | | |
| **Miscellaneous Expense** | | | | | | | | |
| | | | | | | | | |
| **EXPENSES SUBTOTAL:** | | | | | | | | |
| | | | | | | | | |
| **CURRENTLY IN SAVING ACCOUNT:** | | | | | | | | |
| | | | | | | | | |
| **REMAIN IN CHECKING ACCOUNT:** | | | | | | | | |

# Basic Budget Work Sheet

| CATEGORY | Date Started: |
|---|---|
| **INCOME:** | |
| Wages (pay) | |
| Bonuses | |
| Interest income | |
| Capital gain income | |
| Miscellaneous income (for example: child support) | |
| INCOME SUBTOTAL: | |

*(YOUR SUBTOTAL WILL BECOME YOUR INCREASE AFTER YOU ADD UP YOUR INCOME.)*

| EXPENSES: | $ COST | DUE DATE | PAID | PARTIALLY PAID | NEED TO BE PAID ($ BALANCE) | TIME & DATE | REFERENCE/CONFIRMATION NUMBER | SUBTOTAL AFTER EACH PAYMENT |
|---|---|---|---|---|---|---|---|---|
| | | | | | | | | |
| Tithe | 10% | | | | | | | |
| Mortgage, Rent or Lease | | | | | | | | |
| Utilities: Gas/Water/Trash | | | | | | | | |
| Electricity | | | | | | | | |
| Telephone | | | | | | | | |
| Home: Repairs/Maintenance | | | | | | | | |
| Car(s)/Vehicle(s) Payment(s) | | | | | | | | |
| Entertainment | | | | | | | | |
| Auto Insurance | | | | | | | | |
| Transportation Maintenance/Repair | | | | | | | | |
| Vehicle(s) Gasoline | | | | | | | | |
| Child Care/Day Care | | | | | | | | |
| Groceries | | | | | | | | |

| | | | | | | | |
|---|---|---|---|---|---|---|---|
| **Other Transportation: Tolls, Bus, Subway, Etc.** | | | | | | | |
| **Toiletries/Household Products** | | | | | | | |
| **Allowance(s)** | | | | | | | |
| **College Tuition** | | | | | | | |
| **Clothing** | | | | | | | |
| **Eating Out** | | | | | | | |
| **Personal Property Tax** | | | | | | | |
| **Pets (Food and Care)** | | | | | | | |
| **Saving(s)** | | | | | | | |
| **Hobbies** | | | | | | | |
| **Gift(s)/Donation(s)** | | | | | | | |
| **Entertainment/Recreation** | | | | | | | |
| **Credit Card Payment(s)** | | | | | | | |
| **Health Care** | | | | | | | |
| **Emergency** | | | | | | | |
| **Dental** | | | | | | | |
| **Vision** | | | | | | | |
| **Miscellaneous Expense** | | | | | | | |
| **Miscellaneous Expense** | | | | | | | |
| **Miscellaneous Expense** | | | | | | | |
| | | | | | | | |
| **EXPENSES SUBTOTAL:** | | | | | | | |
| | | | | | | | |
| **CURRENTLY IN SAVING ACCOUNT:** | | | | | | | |
| | | | | | | | |
| **REMAIN IN CHECKING ACCOUNT:** | | | | | | | |

# BASIC BUDGET WORK SHEET

| CATEGORY | Date Started: |
|---|---|
| **INCOME:** | |
| Wages (pay) | |
| Bonuses | |
| Interest income | |
| Capital gain income | |
| Miscellaneous income (for example: child support) | |
| **INCOME SUBTOTAL:** | |

*(YOUR SUBTOTAL WILL BECOME YOUR INCREASE AFTER YOU ADD UP YOUR INCOME.)*

| EXPENSES: | $ COST | DUE DATE | PAID | PARTIALLY PAID | NEED TO BE PAID ($ BALANCE) | TIME & DATE | REFERENCE/CON FIRMATION NUMBER | SUBTOTAL AFTER EACH PAYMENT |
|---|---|---|---|---|---|---|---|---|
| | | | | | | | | |
| Tithe | 10% | | | | | | | |
| Mortgage, Rent or Lease | | | | | | | | |
| Utilities: Gas/Water/ Trash | | | | | | | | |
| Electricity | | | | | | | | |
| Telephone | | | | | | | | |
| Home: Repairs/Maintenance | | | | | | | | |
| Car(s)/Vehicle(s) Payment(s) | | | | | | | | |
| Entertainment | | | | | | | | |
| Auto Insurance | | | | | | | | |
| Transportation Maintenance/Repair | | | | | | | | |
| Vehicle(s) Gasoline | | | | | | | | |
| Child Care/Day Care | | | | | | | | |
| Groceries | | | | | | | | |

| | | | | | | | | |
|---|---|---|---|---|---|---|---|---|
| **Other Transportation: Tolls, Bus, Subway, Etc.** | | | | | | | | |
| **Toiletries/Household Products** | | | | | | | | |
| **Allowance(s)** | | | | | | | | |
| **College Tuition** | | | | | | | | |
| **Clothing** | | | | | | | | |
| **Eating Out** | | | | | | | | |
| **Personal Property Tax** | | | | | | | | |
| **Pets (Food and Care)** | | | | | | | | |
| **Saving(s)** | | | | | | | | |
| **Hobbies** | | | | | | | | |
| **Gift(s)/Donation(s)** | | | | | | | | |
| **Entertainment/Recreation** | | | | | | | | |
| **Credit Card Payment(s)** | | | | | | | | |
| **Health Care** | | | | | | | | |
| **Emergency** | | | | | | | | |
| **Dental** | | | | | | | | |
| **Vision** | | | | | | | | |
| **Miscellaneous Expense** | | | | | | | | |
| **Miscellaneous Expense** | | | | | | | | |
| **Miscellaneous Expense** | | | | | | | | |
| | | | | | | | | |
| **EXPENSES SUBTOTAL:** | | | | | | | | |
| | | | | | | | | |
| **CURRENTLY IN SAVING ACCOUNT:** | | | | | | | | |
| | | | | | | | | |
| **REMAIN IN CHECKING ACCOUNT:** | | | | | | | | |

# BASIC BUDGET WORK SHEET

| CATEGORY | Date Started: |
|---|---|
| **INCOME:** | |
| Wages (pay) | |
| Bonuses | |
| Interest income | |
| Capital gain income | |
| Miscellaneous income (for example: child support) | |
| INCOME SUBTOTAL: | |
| *(YOUR SUBTOTAL WILL BECOME YOUR INCREASE AFTER YOU ADD UP YOUR INCOME.)* | |

| EXPENSES: | $ COST | DUE DATE | PAID | PARTIALLY PAID | NEED TO BE PAID ($ BALANCE) | TIME & DATE | REFERENCE/CON FIRMATION NUMBER | SUBTOTAL AFTER EACH PAYMENT |
|---|---|---|---|---|---|---|---|---|
| | | | | | | | | |
| Tithe | 10% | | | | | | | |
| Mortgage, Rent or Lease | | | | | | | | |
| Utilities: Gas/Water/Trash | | | | | | | | |
| Electricity | | | | | | | | |
| Telephone | | | | | | | | |
| Home: Repairs/Maintenance | | | | | | | | |
| Car(s)/Vehicle(s) Payment(s) | | | | | | | | |
| Entertainment | | | | | | | | |
| Auto Insurance | | | | | | | | |
| Transportation Maintenance/Repair | | | | | | | | |
| Vehicle(s) Gasoline | | | | | | | | |
| Child Care/Day Care | | | | | | | | |
| Groceries | | | | | | | | |

| | | | | | | | | |
|---|---|---|---|---|---|---|---|---|
| **Other Transportation: Tolls, Bus, Subway, Etc.** | | | | | | | | |
| **Toiletries/Household Products** | | | | | | | | |
| **Allowance(s)** | | | | | | | | |
| **College Tuition** | | | | | | | | |
| **Clothing** | | | | | | | | |
| **Eating Out** | | | | | | | | |
| **Personal Property Tax** | | | | | | | | |
| **Pets (Food and Care)** | | | | | | | | |
| **Saving(s)** | | | | | | | | |
| **Hobbies** | | | | | | | | |
| **Gift(s)/Donation(s)** | | | | | | | | |
| **Entertainment/Recreation** | | | | | | | | |
| **Credit Card Payment(s)** | | | | | | | | |
| **Health Care** | | | | | | | | |
| **Emergency** | | | | | | | | |
| **Dental** | | | | | | | | |
| **Vision** | | | | | | | | |
| **Miscellaneous Expense** | | | | | | | | |
| **Miscellaneous Expense** | | | | | | | | |
| **Miscellaneous Expense** | | | | | | | | |
| | | | | | | | | |
| **EXPENSES SUBTOTAL:** | | | | | | | | |
| | | | | | | | | |
| **CURRENTLY IN SAVING ACCOUNT:** | | | | | | | | |
| | | | | | | | | |
| **REMAIN IN CHECKING ACCOUNT:** | | | | | | | | |

# BASIC BUDGET WORK SHEET

| CATEGORY | Date Started: |
|---|---|
| **INCOME:** | |
| Wages (pay) | |
| Bonuses | |
| Interest income | |
| Capital gain income | |
| Miscellaneous income (for example: child support) | |
| INCOME SUBTOTAL: | |
| *(YOUR SUBTOTAL WILL BECOME YOUR INCREASE AFTER YOU ADD UP YOUR INCOME.)* | |

| EXPENSES: | $ COST | DUE DATE | PAID | PARTIALLY PAID | NEED TO BE PAID ($ BALANCE) | TIME & DATE | REFERENCE/CON FIRMATION NUMBER | SUBTOTAL AFTER EACH PAYMENT |
|---|---|---|---|---|---|---|---|---|
| | | | | | | | | |
| Tithe | 10% | | | | | | | |
| Mortgage, Rent or Lease | | | | | | | | |
| Utilities: Gas/Water/Trash | | | | | | | | |
| Electricity | | | | | | | | |
| Telephone | | | | | | | | |
| Home: Repairs/Maintenance | | | | | | | | |
| Car(s)/Vehicle(s) Payment(s) | | | | | | | | |
| Entertainment | | | | | | | | |
| Auto Insurance | | | | | | | | |
| Transportation Maintenance/Repair | | | | | | | | |
| Vehicle(s) Gasoline | | | | | | | | |
| Child Care/Day Care | | | | | | | | |
| Groceries | | | | | | | | |

| | | | | | | | | |
|---|---|---|---|---|---|---|---|---|
| **Other Transportation: Tolls, Bus, Subway, Etc.** | | | | | | | | |
| **Toiletries/Household Products** | | | | | | | | |
| **Allowance(s)** | | | | | | | | |
| **College Tuition** | | | | | | | | |
| **Clothing** | | | | | | | | |
| **Eating Out** | | | | | | | | |
| **Personal Property Tax** | | | | | | | | |
| **Pets (Food and Care)** | | | | | | | | |
| **Saving(s)** | | | | | | | | |
| **Hobbies** | | | | | | | | |
| **Gift(s)/Donation(s)** | | | | | | | | |
| **Entertainment/Recreation** | | | | | | | | |
| **Credit Card Payment(s)** | | | | | | | | |
| **Health Care** | | | | | | | | |
| **Emergency** | | | | | | | | |
| **Dental** | | | | | | | | |
| **Vision** | | | | | | | | |
| **Miscellaneous Expense** | | | | | | | | |
| **Miscellaneous Expense** | | | | | | | | |
| **Miscellaneous Expense** | | | | | | | | |
| | | | | | | | | |
| **EXPENSES SUBTOTAL:** | | | | | | | | |
| | | | | | | | | |
| **CURRENTLY IN SAVING ACCOUNT:** | | | | | | | | |
| | | | | | | | | |
| **REMAIN IN CHECKING ACCOUNT:** | | | | | | | | |

# Basic Budget Work Sheet

| CATEGORY | Date Started: |
|---|---|
| **INCOME:** | |
| Wages (pay) | |
| Bonuses | |
| Interest income | |
| Capital gain income | |
| Miscellaneous income (for example: child support) | |
| INCOME SUBTOTAL: | |

*(YOUR SUBTOTAL WILL BECOME YOUR INCREASE AFTER YOU ADD UP YOUR INCOME.)*

| EXPENSES: | $ COST | DUE DATE | PAID | PARTIALLY PAID | NEED TO BE PAID ($ BALANCE) | TIME & DATE | REFERENCE/CON FIRMATION NUMBER | SUBTOTAL AFTER EACH PAYMENT |
|---|---|---|---|---|---|---|---|---|
| | | | | | | | | |
| Tithe | 10% | | | | | | | |
| Mortgage, Rent or Lease | | | | | | | | |
| Utilities: Gas/Water/ Trash | | | | | | | | |
| Electricity | | | | | | | | |
| Telephone | | | | | | | | |
| Home: Repairs/Maintenance | | | | | | | | |
| Car(s)/Vehicle(s) Payment(s) | | | | | | | | |
| Entertainment | | | | | | | | |
| Auto Insurance | | | | | | | | |
| Transportation Maintenance/Repair | | | | | | | | |
| Vehicle(s) Gasoline | | | | | | | | |
| Child Care/Day Care | | | | | | | | |
| Groceries | | | | | | | | |

| | | | | | | | | |
|---|---|---|---|---|---|---|---|---|
| **Other Transportation: Tolls, Bus, Subway, Etc.** | | | | | | | | |
| **Toiletries/Household Products** | | | | | | | | |
| **Allowance(s)** | | | | | | | | |
| **College Tuition** | | | | | | | | |
| **Clothing** | | | | | | | | |
| **Eating Out** | | | | | | | | |
| **Personal Property Tax** | | | | | | | | |
| **Pets (Food and Care)** | | | | | | | | |
| **Saving(s)** | | | | | | | | |
| **Hobbies** | | | | | | | | |
| **Gift(s)/Donation(s)** | | | | | | | | |
| **Entertainment/Recreation** | | | | | | | | |
| **Credit Card Payment(s)** | | | | | | | | |
| **Health Care** | | | | | | | | |
| **Emergency** | | | | | | | | |
| **Dental** | | | | | | | | |
| **Vision** | | | | | | | | |
| **Miscellaneous Expense** | | | | | | | | |
| **Miscellaneous Expense** | | | | | | | | |
| **Miscellaneous Expense** | | | | | | | | |
| | | | | | | | | |
| **EXPENSES SUBTOTAL:** | | | | | | | | |
| | | | | | | | | |
| **CURRENTLY IN SAVING ACCOUNT:** | | | | | | | | |
| | | | | | | | | |
| **REMAIN IN CHECKING ACCOUNT:** | | | | | | | | |

# BASIC BUDGET WORK SHEET

| CATEGORY | Date Started: _____ |
|---|---|
| **INCOME:** | |
| Wages (pay) | |
| Bonuses | |
| Interest income | |
| Capital gain income | |
| Miscellaneous income (for example: child support) | |
| INCOME SUBTOTAL: | |

*(YOUR SUBTOTAL WILL BECOME YOUR INCREASE AFTER YOU ADD UP YOUR INCOME.)*

| EXPENSES: | $ COST | DUE DATE | PAID | PARTIALLY PAID | NEED TO BE PAID ($ BALANCE) | TIME & DATE | REFERENCE/CONFIRMATION NUMBER | SUBTOTAL AFTER EACH PAYMENT |
|---|---|---|---|---|---|---|---|---|
| | | | | | | | | |
| Tithe | 10% | | | | | | | |
| Mortgage, Rent or Lease | | | | | | | | |
| Utilities: Gas/Water/Trash | | | | | | | | |
| Electricity | | | | | | | | |
| Telephone | | | | | | | | |
| Home: Repairs/Maintenance | | | | | | | | |
| Car(s)/Vehicle(s) Payment(s) | | | | | | | | |
| Entertainment | | | | | | | | |
| Auto Insurance | | | | | | | | |
| Transportation Maintenance/Repair | | | | | | | | |
| Vehicle(s) Gasoline | | | | | | | | |
| Child Care/Day Care | | | | | | | | |
| Groceries | | | | | | | | |

| | | | | | | | | |
|---|---|---|---|---|---|---|---|---|
| **Other Transportation: Tolls, Bus, Subway, Etc.** | | | | | | | | |
| **Toiletries/Household Products** | | | | | | | | |
| **Allowance(s)** | | | | | | | | |
| **College Tuition** | | | | | | | | |
| **Clothing** | | | | | | | | |
| **Eating Out** | | | | | | | | |
| **Personal Property Tax** | | | | | | | | |
| **Pets (Food and Care)** | | | | | | | | |
| **Saving(s)** | | | | | | | | |
| **Hobbies** | | | | | | | | |
| **Gift(s)/Donation(s)** | | | | | | | | |
| **Entertainment/Recreation** | | | | | | | | |
| **Credit Card Payment(s)** | | | | | | | | |
| **Health Care** | | | | | | | | |
| **Emergency** | | | | | | | | |
| **Dental** | | | | | | | | |
| **Vision** | | | | | | | | |
| **Miscellaneous Expense** | | | | | | | | |
| **Miscellaneous Expense** | | | | | | | | |
| **Miscellaneous Expense** | | | | | | | | |
| | | | | | | | | |
| **EXPENSES SUBTOTAL:** | | | | | | | | |
| | | | | | | | | |
| **CURRENTLY IN SAVING ACCOUNT:** | | | | | | | | |
| | | | | | | | | |
| **REMAIN IN CHECKING ACCOUNT:** | | | | | | | | |

# Basic Budget Work Sheet

| CATEGORY | Date Started: |
|---|---|
| INCOME: | |

| | |
|---|---|
| Wages (pay) | |
| Bonuses | |
| Interest income | |
| Capital gain income | |
| Miscellaneous income (for example: child support) | |
| INCOME SUBTOTAL: | |

*(YOUR SUBTOTAL WILL BECOME YOUR INCREASE AFTER YOU ADD UP YOUR INCOME.)*

| EXPENSES: | $ COST | DUE DATE | PAID | PARTIALLY PAID | NEED TO BE PAID ($ BALANCE) | TIME & DATE | REFERENCE/CONFIRMATION NUMBER | SUBTOTAL AFTER EACH PAYMENT |
|---|---|---|---|---|---|---|---|---|
| | | | | | | | | |
| Tithe | 10% | | | | | | | |
| Mortgage, Rent or Lease | | | | | | | | |
| Utilities: Gas/Water/Trash | | | | | | | | |
| Electricity | | | | | | | | |
| Telephone | | | | | | | | |
| Home: Repairs/Maintenance | | | | | | | | |
| Car(s)/Vehicle(s) Payment(s) | | | | | | | | |
| Entertainment | | | | | | | | |
| Auto Insurance | | | | | | | | |
| Transportation Maintenance/Repair | | | | | | | | |
| Vehicle(s) Gasoline | | | | | | | | |
| Child Care/Day Care | | | | | | | | |
| Groceries | | | | | | | | |

| | | | | | | | | |
|---|---|---|---|---|---|---|---|---|
| **Other Transportation: Tolls, Bus, Subway, Etc.** | | | | | | | | |
| **Toiletries/Household Products** | | | | | | | | |
| **Allowance(s)** | | | | | | | | |
| **College Tuition** | | | | | | | | |
| **Clothing** | | | | | | | | |
| **Eating Out** | | | | | | | | |
| **Personal Property Tax** | | | | | | | | |
| **Pets (Food and Care)** | | | | | | | | |
| **Saving(s)** | | | | | | | | |
| **Hobbies** | | | | | | | | |
| **Gift(s)/Donation(s)** | | | | | | | | |
| **Entertainment/Recreation** | | | | | | | | |
| **Credit Card Payment(s)** | | | | | | | | |
| **Health Care** | | | | | | | | |
| **Emergency** | | | | | | | | |
| **Dental** | | | | | | | | |
| **Vision** | | | | | | | | |
| **Miscellaneous Expense** | | | | | | | | |
| **Miscellaneous Expense** | | | | | | | | |
| **Miscellaneous Expense** | | | | | | | | |
| | | | | | | | | |
| **EXPENSES SUBTOTAL:** | | | | | | | | |
| | | | | | | | | |
| **CURRENTLY IN SAVING ACCOUNT:** | | | | | | | | |
| | | | | | | | | |
| **REMAIN IN CHECKING ACCOUNT:** | | | | | | | | |

# Basic Budget Work Sheet

| Category | Date Started: _____ |
|---|---|
| **INCOME:** | |
| Wages (pay) | |
| Bonuses | |
| Interest income | |
| Capital gain income | |
| Miscellaneous income (for example: child support) | |
| INCOME SUBTOTAL: | |

*(YOUR SUBTOTAL WILL BECOME YOUR INCREASE AFTER YOU ADD UP YOUR INCOME.)*

| EXPENSES: | $ COST | DUE DATE | PAID | PARTIALLY PAID | NEED TO BE PAID ($ BALANCE) | TIME & DATE | REFERENCE/CONFIRMATION NUMBER | SUBTOTAL AFTER EACH PAYMENT |
|---|---|---|---|---|---|---|---|---|
| | | | | | | | | |
| Tithe | 10% | | | | | | | |
| Mortgage, Rent or Lease | | | | | | | | |
| Utilities: Gas/Water/Trash | | | | | | | | |
| Electricity | | | | | | | | |
| Telephone | | | | | | | | |
| Home: Repairs/Maintenance | | | | | | | | |
| Car(s)/Vehicle(s) Payment(s) | | | | | | | | |
| Entertainment | | | | | | | | |
| Auto Insurance | | | | | | | | |
| Transportation Maintenance/Repair | | | | | | | | |
| Vehicle(s) Gasoline | | | | | | | | |
| Child Care/Day Care | | | | | | | | |
| Groceries | | | | | | | | |

| | | | | | | | |
|---|---|---|---|---|---|---|---|
| **Other Transportation: Tolls, Bus, Subway, Etc.** | | | | | | | |
| **Toiletries/Household Products** | | | | | | | |
| **Allowance(s)** | | | | | | | |
| **College Tuition** | | | | | | | |
| **Clothing** | | | | | | | |
| **Eating Out** | | | | | | | |
| **Personal Property Tax** | | | | | | | |
| **Pets (Food and Care)** | | | | | | | |
| **Saving(s)** | | | | | | | |
| **Hobbies** | | | | | | | |
| **Gift(s)/Donation(s)** | | | | | | | |
| **Entertainment/Recreation** | | | | | | | |
| **Credit Card Payment(s)** | | | | | | | |
| **Health Care** | | | | | | | |
| **Emergency** | | | | | | | |
| **Dental** | | | | | | | |
| **Vision** | | | | | | | |
| **Miscellaneous Expense** | | | | | | | |
| **Miscellaneous Expense** | | | | | | | |
| **Miscellaneous Expense** | | | | | | | |
| | | | | | | | |
| **EXPENSES SUBTOTAL:** | | | | | | | |
| | | | | | | | |
| **CURRENTLY IN SAVING ACCOUNT:** | | | | | | | |
| | | | | | | | |
| **REMAIN IN CHECKING ACCOUNT:** | | | | | | | |

# BASIC BUDGET WORK SHEET

| CATEGORY | Date Started: _____ |
|---|---|
| **INCOME:** | |
| | |
| Wages (pay) | |
| Bonuses | |
| Interest income | |
| Capital gain income | |
| Miscellaneous income (for example: child support) | |
| INCOME SUBTOTAL: | |
| *(YOUR SUBTOTAL WILL BECOME YOUR INCREASE AFTER YOU ADD UP YOUR INCOME.)* | |

| EXPENSES: | $ COST | DUE DATE | PAID | PARTIALLY PAID | NEED TO BE PAID ($ BALANCE) | TIME & DATE | REFERENCE/CONFIRMATION NUMBER | SUBTOTAL AFTER EACH PAYMENT |
|---|---|---|---|---|---|---|---|---|
| | | | | | | | | |
| Tithe | 10% | | | | | | | |
| Mortgage, Rent or Lease | | | | | | | | |
| Utilities: Gas/Water/Trash | | | | | | | | |
| Electricity | | | | | | | | |
| Telephone | | | | | | | | |
| Home: Repairs/Maintenance | | | | | | | | |
| Car(s)/Vehicle(s) Payment(s) | | | | | | | | |
| Entertainment | | | | | | | | |
| Auto Insurance | | | | | | | | |
| Transportation Maintenance/Repair | | | | | | | | |
| Vehicle(s) Gasoline | | | | | | | | |
| Child Care/Day Care | | | | | | | | |
| Groceries | | | | | | | | |

| | | | | | | | | |
|---|---|---|---|---|---|---|---|---|
| **Other Transportation: Tolls, Bus, Subway, Etc.** | | | | | | | | |
| **Toiletries/Household Products** | | | | | | | | |
| **Allowance(s)** | | | | | | | | |
| **College Tuition** | | | | | | | | |
| **Clothing** | | | | | | | | |
| **Eating Out** | | | | | | | | |
| **Personal Property Tax** | | | | | | | | |
| **Pets (Food and Care)** | | | | | | | | |
| **Saving(s)** | | | | | | | | |
| **Hobbies** | | | | | | | | |
| **Gift(s)/Donation(s)** | | | | | | | | |
| **Entertainment/Recreation** | | | | | | | | |
| **Credit Card Payment(s)** | | | | | | | | |
| **Health Care** | | | | | | | | |
| **Emergency** | | | | | | | | |
| **Dental** | | | | | | | | |
| **Vision** | | | | | | | | |
| **Miscellaneous Expense** | | | | | | | | |
| **Miscellaneous Expense** | | | | | | | | |
| **Miscellaneous Expense** | | | | | | | | |
| | | | | | | | | |
| **EXPENSES SUBTOTAL:** | | | | | | | | |
| | | | | | | | | |
| **CURRENTLY IN SAVING ACCOUNT:** | | | | | | | | |
| | | | | | | | | |
| **REMAIN IN CHECKING ACCOUNT:** | | | | | | | | |

# Basic Budget Work Sheet

| CATEGORY | Date Started: _____ |
|---|---|
| **INCOME:** | |
| Wages (pay) | |
| Bonuses | |
| Interest income | |
| Capital gain income | |
| Miscellaneous income (for example: child support) | |
| INCOME SUBTOTAL: | |
| *(YOUR SUBTOTAL WILL BECOME YOUR INCREASE AFTER YOU ADD UP YOUR INCOME.)* | |

| EXPENSES: | $ COST | DUE DATE | PAID | PARTIALLY PAID | NEED TO BE PAID ($ BALANCE) | TIME & DATE | REFERENCE/CON FIRMATION NUMBER | SUBTOTAL AFTER EACH PAYMENT |
|---|---|---|---|---|---|---|---|---|
| | | | | | | | | |
| Tithe | 10% | | | | | | | |
| Mortgage, Rent or Lease | | | | | | | | |
| Utilities: Gas/Water/ Trash | | | | | | | | |
| Electricity | | | | | | | | |
| Telephone | | | | | | | | |
| Home: Repairs/Maintenance | | | | | | | | |
| Car(s)/Vehicle(s) Payment(s) | | | | | | | | |
| Entertainment | | | | | | | | |
| Auto Insurance | | | | | | | | |
| Transportation Maintenance/Repair | | | | | | | | |
| Vehicle(s) Gasoline | | | | | | | | |
| Child Care/Day Care | | | | | | | | |
| Groceries | | | | | | | | |

| | | | | | | | | |
|---|---|---|---|---|---|---|---|---|
| **Other Transportation: Tolls, Bus, Subway, Etc.** | | | | | | | | |
| **Toiletries/Household Products** | | | | | | | | |
| **Allowance(s)** | | | | | | | | |
| **College Tuition** | | | | | | | | |
| **Clothing** | | | | | | | | |
| **Eating Out** | | | | | | | | |
| **Personal Property Tax** | | | | | | | | |
| **Pets (Food and Care)** | | | | | | | | |
| **Saving(s)** | | | | | | | | |
| **Hobbies** | | | | | | | | |
| **Gift(s)/Donation(s)** | | | | | | | | |
| **Entertainment/Recreation** | | | | | | | | |
| **Credit Card Payment(s)** | | | | | | | | |
| **Health Care** | | | | | | | | |
| **Emergency** | | | | | | | | |
| **Dental** | | | | | | | | |
| **Vision** | | | | | | | | |
| **Miscellaneous Expense** | | | | | | | | |
| **Miscellaneous Expense** | | | | | | | | |
| **Miscellaneous Expense** | | | | | | | | |
| | | | | | | | | |
| **EXPENSES SUBTOTAL:** | | | | | | | | |
| | | | | | | | | |
| **CURRENTLY IN SAVING ACCOUNT:** | | | | | | | | |
| | | | | | | | | |
| **REMAIN IN CHECKING ACCOUNT:** | | | | | | | | |

# Basic Budget Work Sheet

| CATEGORY | Date Started: |
|---|---|
| **INCOME:** | |
| Wages (pay) | |
| Bonuses | |
| Interest income | |
| Capital gain income | |
| Miscellaneous income (for example: child support) | |
| INCOME SUBTOTAL: | |
| *(YOUR SUBTOTAL WILL BECOME YOUR INCREASE AFTER YOU ADD UP YOUR INCOME.)* | |

| EXPENSES: | $ COST | DUE DATE | PAID | PARTIALLY PAID | NEED TO BE PAID ($ BALANCE) | TIME & DATE | REFERENCE/CONFIRMATION NUMBER | SUBTOTAL AFTER EACH PAYMENT |
|---|---|---|---|---|---|---|---|---|
| | | | | | | | | |
| Tithe | 10% | | | | | | | |
| Mortgage, Rent or Lease | | | | | | | | |
| Utilities: Gas/Water/ Trash | | | | | | | | |
| Electricity | | | | | | | | |
| Telephone | | | | | | | | |
| Home: Repairs/Maintenance | | | | | | | | |
| Car(s)/Vehicle(s) Payment(s) | | | | | | | | |
| Entertainment | | | | | | | | |
| Auto Insurance | | | | | | | | |
| Transportation Maintenance/Repair | | | | | | | | |
| Vehicle(s) Gasoline | | | | | | | | |
| Child Care/Day Care | | | | | | | | |
| Groceries | | | | | | | | |

| | | | | | | | | |
|---|---|---|---|---|---|---|---|---|
| **Other Transportation: Tolls, Bus, Subway, Etc.** | | | | | | | | |
| **Toiletries/Household Products** | | | | | | | | |
| **Allowance(s)** | | | | | | | | |
| **College Tuition** | | | | | | | | |
| **Clothing** | | | | | | | | |
| **Eating Out** | | | | | | | | |
| **Personal Property Tax** | | | | | | | | |
| **Pets (Food and Care)** | | | | | | | | |
| **Saving(s)** | | | | | | | | |
| **Hobbies** | | | | | | | | |
| **Gift(s)/Donation(s)** | | | | | | | | |
| **Entertainment/Recreation** | | | | | | | | |
| **Credit Card Payment(s)** | | | | | | | | |
| **Health Care** | | | | | | | | |
| **Emergency** | | | | | | | | |
| **Dental** | | | | | | | | |
| **Vision** | | | | | | | | |
| **Miscellaneous Expense** | | | | | | | | |
| **Miscellaneous Expense** | | | | | | | | |
| **Miscellaneous Expense** | | | | | | | | |
| | | | | | | | | |
| **EXPENSES SUBTOTAL:** | | | | | | | | |
| | | | | | | | | |
| **CURRENTLY IN SAVING ACCOUNT:** | | | | | | | | |
| | | | | | | | | |
| **REMAIN IN CHECKING ACCOUNT:** | | | | | | | | |

# Basic Budget Work Sheet

| CATEGORY | Date Started: |
|---|---|
| **INCOME:** | |
| Wages (pay) | |
| Bonuses | |
| Interest income | |
| Capital gain income | |
| Miscellaneous income (for example: child support) | |
| INCOME SUBTOTAL: | |

*(YOUR SUBTOTAL WILL BECOME YOUR INCREASE AFTER YOU ADD UP YOUR INCOME.)*

| EXPENSES: | $ COST | DUE DATE | PAID | PARTIALLY PAID | NEED TO BE PAID ($ BALANCE) | TIME & DATE | REFERENCE/CONFIRMATION NUMBER | SUBTOTAL AFTER EACH PAYMENT |
|---|---|---|---|---|---|---|---|---|
| | | | | | | | | |
| Tithe | 10% | | | | | | | |
| Mortgage, Rent or Lease | | | | | | | | |
| Utilities: Gas/Water/ Trash | | | | | | | | |
| Electricity | | | | | | | | |
| Telephone | | | | | | | | |
| Home: Repairs/Maintenance | | | | | | | | |
| Car(s)/Vehicle(s) Payment(s) | | | | | | | | |
| Entertainment | | | | | | | | |
| Auto Insurance | | | | | | | | |
| Transportation Maintenance/Repair | | | | | | | | |
| Vehicle(s) Gasoline | | | | | | | | |
| Child Care/Day Care | | | | | | | | |
| Groceries | | | | | | | | |

| | | | | | | | |
|---|---|---|---|---|---|---|---|
| Other Transportation: Tolls, Bus, Subway, Etc. | | | | | | | |
| Toiletries/Household Products | | | | | | | |
| Allowance(s) | | | | | | | |
| College Tuition | | | | | | | |
| Clothing | | | | | | | |
| Eating Out | | | | | | | |
| Personal Property Tax | | | | | | | |
| Pets (Food and Care) | | | | | | | |
| Saving(s) | | | | | | | |
| Hobbies | | | | | | | |
| Gift(s)/Donation(s) | | | | | | | |
| Entertainment/Recreation | | | | | | | |
| Credit Card Payment(s) | | | | | | | |
| Health Care | | | | | | | |
| Emergency | | | | | | | |
| Dental | | | | | | | |
| Vision | | | | | | | |
| Miscellaneous Expense | | | | | | | |
| Miscellaneous Expense | | | | | | | |
| Miscellaneous Expense | | | | | | | |
| | | | | | | | |
| EXPENSES SUBTOTAL: | | | | | | | |
| | | | | | | | |
| CURRENTLY IN SAVING ACCOUNT: | | | | | | | |
| | | | | | | | |
| REMAIN IN CHECKING ACCOUNT: | | | | | | | |

# Basic Budget Work Sheet

| CATEGORY | Date Started: |
|---|---|
| **INCOME:** | |
| Wages (pay) | |
| Bonuses | |
| Interest income | |
| Capital gain income | |
| Miscellaneous income (for example: child support) | |
| **INCOME SUBTOTAL:** | |

*(YOUR SUBTOTAL WILL BECOME YOUR INCREASE AFTER YOU ADD UP YOUR INCOME.)*

| EXPENSES: | $ COST | DUE DATE | PAID | PARTIALLY PAID | NEED TO BE PAID ($ BALANCE) | TIME & DATE | REFERENCE/CON FIRMATION NUMBER | SUBTOTAL AFTER EACH PAYMENT |
|---|---|---|---|---|---|---|---|---|
| | | | | | | | | |
| Tithe | 10% | | | | | | | |
| Mortgage, Rent or Lease | | | | | | | | |
| Utilities: Gas/Water/ Trash | | | | | | | | |
| Electricity | | | | | | | | |
| Telephone | | | | | | | | |
| Home: Repairs/Maintenance | | | | | | | | |
| Car(s)/Vehicle(s) Payment(s) | | | | | | | | |
| Entertainment | | | | | | | | |
| Auto Insurance | | | | | | | | |
| Transportation Maintenance/Repair | | | | | | | | |
| Vehicle(s) Gasoline | | | | | | | | |
| Child Care/Day Care | | | | | | | | |
| Groceries | | | | | | | | |

| | | | | | | | | |
|---|---|---|---|---|---|---|---|---|
| **Other Transportation: Tolls, Bus, Subway, Etc.** | | | | | | | | |
| **Toiletries/Household Products** | | | | | | | | |
| **Allowance(s)** | | | | | | | | |
| **College Tuition** | | | | | | | | |
| **Clothing** | | | | | | | | |
| **Eating Out** | | | | | | | | |
| **Personal Property Tax** | | | | | | | | |
| **Pets (Food and Care)** | | | | | | | | |
| **Saving(s)** | | | | | | | | |
| **Hobbies** | | | | | | | | |
| **Gift(s)/Donation(s)** | | | | | | | | |
| **Entertainment/Recreation** | | | | | | | | |
| **Credit Card Payment(s)** | | | | | | | | |
| **Health Care** | | | | | | | | |
| **Emergency** | | | | | | | | |
| **Dental** | | | | | | | | |
| **Vision** | | | | | | | | |
| **Miscellaneous Expense** | | | | | | | | |
| **Miscellaneous Expense** | | | | | | | | |
| **Miscellaneous Expense** | | | | | | | | |
| | | | | | | | | |
| **EXPENSES SUBTOTAL:** | | | | | | | | |
| | | | | | | | | |
| **CURRENTLY IN SAVING ACCOUNT:** | | | | | | | | |
| | | | | | | | | |
| **REMAIN IN CHECKING ACCOUNT:** | | | | | | | | |

# Basic Budget Work Sheet

| CATEGORY | Date Started: _____ |
|---|---|
| **INCOME:** | |
| Wages (pay) | |
| Bonuses | |
| Interest income | |
| Capital gain income | |
| Miscellaneous income (for example: child support) | |
| **INCOME SUBTOTAL:** | |

*(YOUR SUBTOTAL WILL BECOME YOUR INCREASE AFTER YOU ADD UP YOUR INCOME.)*

| **EXPENSES:** | **$ COST** | **DUE DATE** | **PAID** | **PARTIALLY PAID** | **NEED TO BE PAID ($ BALANCE)** | **TIME & DATE** | **REFERENCE/CONFIRMATION NUMBER** | **SUBTOTAL AFTER EACH PAYMENT** |
|---|---|---|---|---|---|---|---|---|
| | | | | | | | | |
| Tithe | 10% | | | | | | | |
| Mortgage, Rent or Lease | | | | | | | | |
| Utilities: Gas/Water/Trash | | | | | | | | |
| Electricity | | | | | | | | |
| Telephone | | | | | | | | |
| Home: Repairs/Maintenance | | | | | | | | |
| Car(s)/Vehicle(s) Payment(s) | | | | | | | | |
| Entertainment | | | | | | | | |
| Auto Insurance | | | | | | | | |
| Transportation Maintenance/Repair | | | | | | | | |
| Vehicle(s) Gasoline | | | | | | | | |
| Child Care/Day Care | | | | | | | | |
| Groceries | | | | | | | | |

| | | | | | | | |
|---|---|---|---|---|---|---|---|
| Other Transportation: Tolls, Bus, Subway, Etc. | | | | | | | |
| Toiletries/Household Products | | | | | | | |
| Allowance(s) | | | | | | | |
| College Tuition | | | | | | | |
| Clothing | | | | | | | |
| Eating Out | | | | | | | |
| Personal Property Tax | | | | | | | |
| Pets (Food and Care) | | | | | | | |
| Saving(s) | | | | | | | |
| Hobbies | | | | | | | |
| Gift(s)/Donation(s) | | | | | | | |
| Entertainment/Recreation | | | | | | | |
| Credit Card Payment(s) | | | | | | | |
| Health Care | | | | | | | |
| Emergency | | | | | | | |
| Dental | | | | | | | |
| Vision | | | | | | | |
| Miscellaneous Expense | | | | | | | |
| Miscellaneous Expense | | | | | | | |
| Miscellaneous Expense | | | | | | | |
| | | | | | | | |
| EXPENSES SUBTOTAL: | | | | | | | |
| | | | | | | | |
| CURRENTLY IN SAVING ACCOUNT: | | | | | | | |
| | | | | | | | |
| REMAIN IN CHECKING ACCOUNT: | | | | | | | |

# Basic Budget Work Sheet

| Category | Date Started: |
|---|---|
| **INCOME:** | |
| Wages (pay) | |
| Bonuses | |
| Interest income | |
| Capital gain income | |
| Miscellaneous income (for example: child support) | |
| INCOME SUBTOTAL: | |

*(YOUR SUBTOTAL WILL BECOME YOUR INCREASE AFTER YOU ADD UP YOUR INCOME.)*

| EXPENSES: | $ COST | DUE DATE | PAID | PARTIALLY PAID | NEED TO BE PAID ($ BALANCE) | TIME & DATE | REFERENCE/CONFIRMATION NUMBER | SUBTOTAL AFTER EACH PAYMENT |
|---|---|---|---|---|---|---|---|---|
| | | | | | | | | |
| Tithe | 10% | | | | | | | |
| Mortgage, Rent or Lease | | | | | | | | |
| Utilities: Gas/Water/Trash | | | | | | | | |
| Electricity | | | | | | | | |
| Telephone | | | | | | | | |
| Home: Repairs/Maintenance | | | | | | | | |
| Car(s)/Vehicle(s) Payment(s) | | | | | | | | |
| Entertainment | | | | | | | | |
| Auto Insurance | | | | | | | | |
| Transportation Maintenance/Repair | | | | | | | | |
| Vehicle(s) Gasoline | | | | | | | | |
| Child Care/Day Care | | | | | | | | |
| Groceries | | | | | | | | |

| | | | | | | | | |
|---|---|---|---|---|---|---|---|---|
| **Other Transportation: Tolls, Bus, Subway, Etc.** | | | | | | | | |
| **Toiletries/Household Products** | | | | | | | | |
| **Allowance(s)** | | | | | | | | |
| **College Tuition** | | | | | | | | |
| **Clothing** | | | | | | | | |
| **Eating Out** | | | | | | | | |
| **Personal Property Tax** | | | | | | | | |
| **Pets (Food and Care)** | | | | | | | | |
| **Saving(s)** | | | | | | | | |
| **Hobbies** | | | | | | | | |
| **Gift(s)/Donation(s)** | | | | | | | | |
| **Entertainment/Recreation** | | | | | | | | |
| **Credit Card Payment(s)** | | | | | | | | |
| **Health Care** | | | | | | | | |
| **Emergency** | | | | | | | | |
| **Dental** | | | | | | | | |
| **Vision** | | | | | | | | |
| **Miscellaneous Expense** | | | | | | | | |
| **Miscellaneous Expense** | | | | | | | | |
| **Miscellaneous Expense** | | | | | | | | |
| | | | | | | | | |
| **EXPENSES SUBTOTAL:** | | | | | | | | |
| | | | | | | | | |
| **CURRENTLY IN SAVING ACCOUNT:** | | | | | | | | |
| | | | | | | | | |
| **REMAIN IN CHECKING ACCOUNT:** | | | | | | | | |

# BASIC BUDGET WORK SHEET

| CATEGORY | Date Started: |
|---|---|
| **INCOME:** | |
| Wages (pay) | |
| Bonuses | |
| Interest income | |
| Capital gain income | |
| Miscellaneous income (for example: child support) | |
| INCOME SUBTOTAL: | |
| *(YOUR SUBTOTAL WILL BECOME YOUR INCREASE AFTER YOU ADD UP YOUR INCOME.)* | |

| EXPENSES: | $ COST | DUE DATE | PAID | PARTIALLY PAID | NEED TO BE PAID ($ BALANCE) | TIME & DATE | REFERENCE/CONFIRMATION NUMBER | SUBTOTAL AFTER EACH PAYMENT |
|---|---|---|---|---|---|---|---|---|
| | | | | | | | | |
| Tithe | 10% | | | | | | | |
| Mortgage, Rent or Lease | | | | | | | | |
| Utilities: Gas/Water/Trash | | | | | | | | |
| Electricity | | | | | | | | |
| Telephone | | | | | | | | |
| Home: Repairs/Maintenance | | | | | | | | |
| Car(s)/Vehicle(s) Payment(s) | | | | | | | | |
| Entertainment | | | | | | | | |
| Auto Insurance | | | | | | | | |
| Transportation Maintenance/Repair | | | | | | | | |
| Vehicle(s) Gasoline | | | | | | | | |
| Child Care/Day Care | | | | | | | | |
| Groceries | | | | | | | | |

| | | | | | | | | |
|---|---|---|---|---|---|---|---|---|
| **Other Transportation: Tolls, Bus, Subway, Etc.** | | | | | | | | |
| **Toiletries/Household Products** | | | | | | | | |
| **Allowance(s)** | | | | | | | | |
| **College Tuition** | | | | | | | | |
| **Clothing** | | | | | | | | |
| **Eating Out** | | | | | | | | |
| **Personal Property Tax** | | | | | | | | |
| **Pets (Food and Care)** | | | | | | | | |
| **Saving(s)** | | | | | | | | |
| **Hobbies** | | | | | | | | |
| **Gift(s)/Donation(s)** | | | | | | | | |
| **Entertainment/Recreation** | | | | | | | | |
| **Credit Card Payment(s)** | | | | | | | | |
| **Health Care** | | | | | | | | |
| **Emergency** | | | | | | | | |
| **Dental** | | | | | | | | |
| **Vision** | | | | | | | | |
| **Miscellaneous Expense** | | | | | | | | |
| **Miscellaneous Expense** | | | | | | | | |
| **Miscellaneous Expense** | | | | | | | | |
| | | | | | | | | |
| **EXPENSES SUBTOTAL:** | | | | | | | | |
| | | | | | | | | |
| **CURRENTLY IN SAVING ACCOUNT:** | | | | | | | | |
| | | | | | | | | |
| **REMAIN IN CHECKING ACCOUNT:** | | | | | | | | |

# BASIC BUDGET WORK SHEET

| CATEGORY | Date Started: |
|---|---|
| | **INCOME:** |
| Wages (pay) | |
| Bonuses | |
| Interest income | |
| Capital gain income | |
| Miscellaneous income (for example: child support) | |
| INCOME SUBTOTAL: | |

*(YOUR SUBTOTAL WILL BECOME YOUR INCREASE AFTER YOU ADD UP YOUR INCOME.)*

| EXPENSES: | $ COST | DUE DATE | PAID | PARTIALLY PAID | NEED TO BE PAID ($ BALANCE) | TIME & DATE | REFERENCE/CON FIRMATION NUMBER | SUBTOTAL AFTER EACH PAYMENT |
|---|---|---|---|---|---|---|---|---|
| | | | | | | | | |
| Tithe | 10% | | | | | | | |
| Mortgage, Rent or Lease | | | | | | | | |
| Utilities: Gas/Water/Trash | | | | | | | | |
| Electricity | | | | | | | | |
| Telephone | | | | | | | | |
| Home: Repairs/Maintenance | | | | | | | | |
| Car(s)/Vehicle(s) Payment(s) | | | | | | | | |
| Entertainment | | | | | | | | |
| Auto Insurance | | | | | | | | |
| Transportation Maintenance/Repair | | | | | | | | |
| Vehicle(s) Gasoline | | | | | | | | |
| Child Care/Day Care | | | | | | | | |
| Groceries | | | | | | | | |

| | | | | | | | | |
|---|---|---|---|---|---|---|---|---|
| **Other Transportation: Tolls, Bus, Subway, Etc.** | | | | | | | | |
| **Toiletries/Household Products** | | | | | | | | |
| **Allowance(s)** | | | | | | | | |
| **College Tuition** | | | | | | | | |
| **Clothing** | | | | | | | | |
| **Eating Out** | | | | | | | | |
| **Personal Property Tax** | | | | | | | | |
| **Pets (Food and Care)** | | | | | | | | |
| **Saving(s)** | | | | | | | | |
| **Hobbies** | | | | | | | | |
| **Gift(s)/Donation(s)** | | | | | | | | |
| **Entertainment/Recreation** | | | | | | | | |
| **Credit Card Payment(s)** | | | | | | | | |
| **Health Care** | | | | | | | | |
| **Emergency** | | | | | | | | |
| **Dental** | | | | | | | | |
| **Vision** | | | | | | | | |
| **Miscellaneous Expense** | | | | | | | | |
| **Miscellaneous Expense** | | | | | | | | |
| **Miscellaneous Expense** | | | | | | | | |
| | | | | | | | | |
| **EXPENSES SUBTOTAL:** | | | | | | | | |
| | | | | | | | | |
| **CURRENTLY IN SAVING ACCOUNT:** | | | | | | | | |
| | | | | | | | | |
| **REMAIN IN CHECKING ACCOUNT:** | | | | | | | | |

# Basic Budget Work Sheet

| CATEGORY | Date Started:_____ | | | | | | |
|----------|-----|---|---|---|---|---|---|
| | INCOME: | | | | | | |
| Wages (pay) | | | | | | | |
| Bonuses | | | | | | | |
| Interest income | | | | | | | |
| Capital gain income | | | | | | | |
| Miscellaneous income (for example: child support) | | | | | | | |
| INCOME SUBTOTAL: | | | | | | | |

*(YOUR SUBTOTAL WILL BECOME YOUR INCREASE AFTER YOU ADD UP YOUR INCOME.)*

| EXPENSES: | $ COST | DUE DATE | PAID | PARTIALLY PAID | NEED TO BE PAID ($ BALANCE) | TIME & DATE | REFERENCE/CONFIRMATION NUMBER | SUBTOTAL AFTER EACH PAYMENT |
|-----------|--------|----------|------|----------------|------------------------------|-------------|-------------------------------|------------------------------|
| | | | | | | | | |
| Tithe | 10% | | | | | | | |
| Mortgage, Rent or Lease | | | | | | | | |
| Utilities: Gas/Water/Trash | | | | | | | | |
| Electricity | | | | | | | | |
| Telephone | | | | | | | | |
| Home: Repairs/Maintenance | | | | | | | | |
| Car(s)/Vehicle(s) Payment(s) | | | | | | | | |
| Entertainment | | | | | | | | |
| Auto Insurance | | | | | | | | |
| Transportation Maintenance/Repair | | | | | | | | |
| Vehicle(s) Gasoline | | | | | | | | |
| Child Care/Day Care | | | | | | | | |
| Groceries | | | | | | | | |

| | | | | | | | | |
|---|---|---|---|---|---|---|---|---|
| Other Transportation: Tolls, Bus, Subway, Etc. | | | | | | | | |
| Toiletries/Household Products | | | | | | | | |
| Allowance(s) | | | | | | | | |
| College Tuition | | | | | | | | |
| Clothing | | | | | | | | |
| Eating Out | | | | | | | | |
| Personal Property Tax | | | | | | | | |
| Pets (Food and Care) | | | | | | | | |
| Saving(s) | | | | | | | | |
| Hobbies | | | | | | | | |
| Gift(s)/Donation(s) | | | | | | | | |
| Entertainment/Recreation | | | | | | | | |
| Credit Card Payment(s) | | | | | | | | |
| Health Care | | | | | | | | |
| Emergency | | | | | | | | |
| Dental | | | | | | | | |
| Vision | | | | | | | | |
| Miscellaneous Expense | | | | | | | | |
| Miscellaneous Expense | | | | | | | | |
| Miscellaneous Expense | | | | | | | | |
| | | | | | | | | |
| EXPENSES SUBTOTAL: | | | | | | | | |
| | | | | | | | | |
| CURRENTLY IN SAVING ACCOUNT: | | | | | | | | |
| | | | | | | | | |
| REMAIN IN CHECKING ACCOUNT: | | | | | | | | |

# BASIC BUDGET WORK SHEET

| CATEGORY | Date Started: |
|---|---|
| INCOME: | |
| Wages (pay) | |
| Bonuses | |
| Interest income | |
| Capital gain income | |
| Miscellaneous income (for example: child support) | |
| INCOME SUBTOTAL: | |

*(YOUR SUBTOTAL WILL BECOME YOUR INCREASE AFTER YOU ADD UP YOUR INCOME.)*

| EXPENSES: | $ COST | DUE DATE | PAID | PARTIALLY PAID | NEED TO BE PAID ($ BALANCE) | TIME & DATE | REFERENCE/CONFIRMATION NUMBER | SUBTOTAL AFTER EACH PAYMENT |
|---|---|---|---|---|---|---|---|---|
| | | | | | | | | |
| Tithe | 10% | | | | | | | |
| Mortgage, Rent or Lease | | | | | | | | |
| Utilities: Gas/Water/Trash | | | | | | | | |
| Electricity | | | | | | | | |
| Telephone | | | | | | | | |
| Home: Repairs/Maintenance | | | | | | | | |
| Car(s)/Vehicle(s) Payment(s) | | | | | | | | |
| Entertainment | | | | | | | | |
| Auto Insurance | | | | | | | | |
| Transportation Maintenance/Repair | | | | | | | | |
| Vehicle(s) Gasoline | | | | | | | | |
| Child Care/Day Care | | | | | | | | |
| Groceries | | | | | | | | |

| | | | | | | | | |
|---|---|---|---|---|---|---|---|---|
| **Other Transportation: Tolls, Bus, Subway, Etc.** | | | | | | | | |
| **Toiletries/Household Products** | | | | | | | | |
| **Allowance(s)** | | | | | | | | |
| **College Tuition** | | | | | | | | |
| **Clothing** | | | | | | | | |
| **Eating Out** | | | | | | | | |
| **Personal Property Tax** | | | | | | | | |
| **Pets (Food and Care)** | | | | | | | | |
| **Saving(s)** | | | | | | | | |
| **Hobbies** | | | | | | | | |
| **Gift(s)/Donation(s)** | | | | | | | | |
| **Entertainment/Recreation** | | | | | | | | |
| **Credit Card Payment(s)** | | | | | | | | |
| **Health Care** | | | | | | | | |
| **Emergency** | | | | | | | | |
| **Dental** | | | | | | | | |
| **Vision** | | | | | | | | |
| **Miscellaneous Expense** | | | | | | | | |
| **Miscellaneous Expense** | | | | | | | | |
| **Miscellaneous Expense** | | | | | | | | |
| | | | | | | | | |
| **EXPENSES SUBTOTAL:** | | | | | | | | |
| | | | | | | | | |
| **CURRENTLY IN SAVING ACCOUNT:** | | | | | | | | |
| | | | | | | | | |
| **REMAIN IN CHECKING ACCOUNT:** | | | | | | | | |

# BASIC BUDGET WORK SHEET

| CATEGORY | Date Started: _____ |
|---|---|
| **INCOME:** | |

| | |
|---|---|
| Wages (pay) | |
| Bonuses | |
| Interest income | |
| Capital gain income | |
| Miscellaneous income (for example: child support) | |
| INCOME SUBTOTAL: | |

*(YOUR SUBTOTAL WILL BECOME YOUR INCREASE AFTER YOU ADD UP YOUR INCOME.)*

| EXPENSES: | $ COST | DUE DATE | PAID | PARTIALLY PAID | NEED TO BE PAID ($ BALANCE) | TIME & DATE | REFERENCE/CONFIRMATION NUMBER | SUBTOTAL AFTER EACH PAYMENT |
|---|---|---|---|---|---|---|---|---|
| | | | | | | | | |
| Tithe | 10% | | | | | | | |
| Mortgage, Rent or Lease | | | | | | | | |
| Utilities: Gas/Water/ Trash | | | | | | | | |
| Electricity | | | | | | | | |
| Telephone | | | | | | | | |
| Home: Repairs/Maintenance | | | | | | | | |
| Car(s)/Vehicle(s) Payment(s) | | | | | | | | |
| Entertainment | | | | | | | | |
| Auto Insurance | | | | | | | | |
| Transportation Maintenance/Repair | | | | | | | | |
| Vehicle(s) Gasoline | | | | | | | | |
| Child Care/Day Care | | | | | | | | |
| Groceries | | | | | | | | |

| | | | | | | | | |
|---|---|---|---|---|---|---|---|---|
| **Other Transportation: Tolls, Bus, Subway, Etc.** | | | | | | | | |
| **Toiletries/Household Products** | | | | | | | | |
| **Allowance(s)** | | | | | | | | |
| **College Tuition** | | | | | | | | |
| **Clothing** | | | | | | | | |
| **Eating Out** | | | | | | | | |
| **Personal Property Tax** | | | | | | | | |
| **Pets (Food and Care)** | | | | | | | | |
| **Saving(s)** | | | | | | | | |
| **Hobbies** | | | | | | | | |
| **Gift(s)/Donation(s)** | | | | | | | | |
| **Entertainment/Recreation** | | | | | | | | |
| **Credit Card Payment(s)** | | | | | | | | |
| **Health Care** | | | | | | | | |
| **Emergency** | | | | | | | | |
| **Dental** | | | | | | | | |
| **Vision** | | | | | | | | |
| **Miscellaneous Expense** | | | | | | | | |
| **Miscellaneous Expense** | | | | | | | | |
| **Miscellaneous Expense** | | | | | | | | |
| | | | | | | | | |
| **EXPENSES SUBTOTAL:** | | | | | | | | |
| | | | | | | | | |
| **CURRENTLY IN SAVING ACCOUNT:** | | | | | | | | |
| | | | | | | | | |
| **REMAIN IN CHECKING ACCOUNT:** | | | | | | | | |

# BASIC BUDGET WORK SHEET

| CATEGORY | Date Started: _____ |
|---|---|
| INCOME: | |
| Wages (pay) | |
| Bonuses | |
| Interest income | |
| Capital gain income | |
| Miscellaneous income (for example: child support) | |
| INCOME SUBTOTAL: | |
| *(YOUR SUBTOTAL WILL BECOME YOUR INCREASE AFTER YOU ADD UP YOUR INCOME.)* | |

| EXPENSES: | $ COST | DUE DATE | PAID | PARTIALLY PAID | NEED TO BE PAID ($ BALANCE) | TIME & DATE | REFERENCE/CONFIRMATION NUMBER | SUBTOTAL AFTER EACH PAYMENT |
|---|---|---|---|---|---|---|---|---|
| | | | | | | | | |
| Tithe | 10% | | | | | | | |
| Mortgage, Rent or Lease | | | | | | | | |
| Utilities: Gas/Water/ Trash | | | | | | | | |
| Electricity | | | | | | | | |
| Telephone | | | | | | | | |
| Home: Repairs/Maintenance | | | | | | | | |
| Car(s)/Vehicle(s) Payment(s) | | | | | | | | |
| Entertainment | | | | | | | | |
| Auto Insurance | | | | | | | | |
| Transportation Maintenance/Repair | | | | | | | | |
| Vehicle(s) Gasoline | | | | | | | | |
| Child Care/Day Care | | | | | | | | |
| Groceries | | | | | | | | |

| | | | | | | | | |
|---|---|---|---|---|---|---|---|---|
| **Other Transportation: Tolls, Bus, Subway, Etc.** | | | | | | | | |
| **Toiletries/Household Products** | | | | | | | | |
| **Allowance(s)** | | | | | | | | |
| **College Tuition** | | | | | | | | |
| **Clothing** | | | | | | | | |
| **Eating Out** | | | | | | | | |
| **Personal Property Tax** | | | | | | | | |
| **Pets (Food and Care)** | | | | | | | | |
| **Saving(s)** | | | | | | | | |
| **Hobbies** | | | | | | | | |
| **Gift(s)/Donation(s)** | | | | | | | | |
| **Entertainment/Recreation** | | | | | | | | |
| **Credit Card Payment(s)** | | | | | | | | |
| **Health Care** | | | | | | | | |
| **Emergency** | | | | | | | | |
| **Dental** | | | | | | | | |
| **Vision** | | | | | | | | |
| **Miscellaneous Expense** | | | | | | | | |
| **Miscellaneous Expense** | | | | | | | | |
| **Miscellaneous Expense** | | | | | | | | |
| | | | | | | | | |
| **EXPENSES SUBTOTAL:** | | | | | | | | |
| | | | | | | | | |
| **CURRENTLY IN SAVING ACCOUNT:** | | | | | | | | |
| | | | | | | | | |
| **REMAIN IN CHECKING ACCOUNT:** | | | | | | | | |